Home Buying

—Made Easy—

SAVE THOUSANDS OF DOLLARS
WHEN BUYING YOUR NEXT HOME

Alex A. Lluch

Author of Over 3 Million Books Sold

WS Publishing Group
San Diego, California

Home Buying Made Easy

By Alex A. Lluch

Published by WS Publishing Group
San Diego, CA 92119
Copyright © 2009 by WS Publishing Group

All rights reserved under International and Pan-American Copyright conventions. No part of this book may be reproduced or transmitted in any form or by any means, electronic or mechanical, including photocopy, recording or by any information storage and retrieval system, without permission in writing from the publisher.

Designed by WS Publishing Group:
David Defenbaugh and Sarah Jang

Photo Credit: © Mike Seidle/Corbis

For Inquiries:
Log on to www.WSPublishingGroup.com
E-mail info@WSPublishingGroup.com

ISBN 13: 978-1-934386-31-6

Printed in China

place photo
of home here

The home of:

_____

Located at:

_____

Date purchased:

_____

TABLE OF CONTENTS

TABLE OF CONTENTS

TABLE OF CONTENTS

INTRODUCTION

Home Buying Made Easy was designed to guide you through one of the most exciting, satisfying and financially rewarding things you'll do in your lifetime.

This book covers everything from envisioning your dream home to signing the final documents involved in its purchase. Between those two thrilling extremes, you'll learn all about examining current trends to decide exactly where and when you should buy; adding up your assets and liabilities to figure out how much house you can afford; coming up with a down payment; deciding which type of mortgage is right for you; going on home tours; getting the best deal; getting through escrow; and closing the deal. We've gathered all of the tools and information you'll need and combined them in a unique format that's comprehensive and yet easy to follow and understand.

Home Buying Made Easy does more than just provide useful information. It is also packed with checklists, worksheets and other interactive features, so that you can make this book entirely your own! Use this book not only as a source of information, but also as a tool to organize your finances, calculate just how much house you can afford, discover the best type of loan for your family and map out the house of your dreams. Mark it up. Fill out the worksheets, write questions for Realtors in the margins and scribble your comments on the note pages. This is your book! *Home Buying Made Easy* will help you become more informed about the process ... and ultimately help you find and purchase the home that's just right for you.

ABOUT HOME BUYING MADE EASY

Whether you choose to work with a Realtor or venture into the home buying arena on your own, the more informed you are, the more successful you will be. Regardless of what stage of life you're in, as a potential home buyer you must evaluate your finances, go on house tours, secure a mortgage, get through escrow ... and then go through the process of actually moving into another residence. Anyone thinking of buying a house or already in the process of doing so needs this book.

INTRODUCTION

PART 1: ARE YOU READY FOR REAL ESTATE?

Chapter 1: The Ownership Advantage introduces the benefits of homeownership. It offers a side-by-side comparison of owning versus renting, walks you through some good reasons to own your own residence, and even lists some motivations you should steer clear of when considering a home purchase.

Chapter 2: Is This the Right Time to Buy? asks you to consider issues such as the current housing market, population trends and your own personal long-range vision. The information provided in this first section of the book should prompt some self analysis on your part.

PART 2: HOW MUCH HOUSE CAN YOU AFFORD?

Chapter 3: Understanding How Much You Can Afford takes an honest look at your financial situation and home buying potential.

Chapter 4: Your Credit Report discusses the international computerized organizations that keep track of how you pay your bills. We'll explain credit reports and credit scores, and tell you what credit score you'll need to get a home loan. If you're unhappy with what appears on your report, we'll explain ways that you can improve, fix and strengthen it.

Chapter 5: Information Your Lender Will Require helps you get organized prior to meeting with your lender. There's a checklist, some questions to ask and a rundown of documents you'll need to bring with you.

Chapter 6: The Down Payment suggests ways to fund your initial outlay of cash and includes descriptions of government resources set up to assist you in doing so. A worksheet that tracks your down payment sources helps you add it all up.

PART 3: ALL ABOUT FINANCING

Chapter 7: Understanding the Mortgage Process answers the home buyer's most pressing question: How much money will the bank let me borrow? Further, this chapter will help you decide whether you want to borrow the very maximum the bank will allow or have a low enough mortgage to put a decent amount of money into your tax-free retirement account.

Chapter 8: Fixed Rate Mortgages compares the advantages and disadvantages of this type of financing. A worksheet keeps track of things like interest and monthly payments, while our mortgage calculator shows how the numbers add up.

Chapter 9: Adjustable Rate Mortgages takes a look at ARMs, offers tips on adjusting for peaks and valleys and provides questions to ask your mortgage lender about this type of financing.

Chapter 10: Other Home Financing Options explores some nonconventional choices such as seller financing, interest-only loans and two-step mortgages.

PART 4: FINDING YOUR DREAM HOME

In *Chapter 11: What Makes a House a Dream Home*, you can go over just what really does matter to you and what you can live without both now and five to ten years down the road. With the worksheets provided, you and your spouse or partner can compare priorities and hash them out before you involve an agent.

Chapter 12: Buying a Condominium discusses this popular alternative to investing in a home.

Chapter 13: Tips on Getting a Good Deal shows how buying a fixer-upper, buying in a gloomy economy and buying in unproven neighborhoods are just a few ways you can find hidden bargains.

Chapter 14: Choosing a Realtor gives you the signs of a good agent, a list of questions to ask potential agents and other information to keep you in the driver's seat in the agent/client relationship.

Chapter 15: Inspecting Your Home lists tips that will not only help your home inspection go smoothly, but also make sure every needed repair in your new home is found and addressed.

Chapter 16: Disclosure discusses items to watch in a disclosure statement and tells how to reject a property because of disclosure. It also provides a sample disclosure form.

PART 5: NEGOTIATING LIKE THE PROS

Chapter 17: Secrets of Winning Negotiations emphasizes that the more you know and understand about the financial aspects of a purchase this large, the more enjoyable and rewarding the whole process will be. This chapter takes you through all the steps, from evaluating the asking price to handling a multi-bid situation.

PART 6: MAKING THE PURCHASE

Chapter 18: Closing Time – Getting Through Escrow teaches you that though the end is in sight, there are still inspections to schedule, documents to gather, signings to attend and monies to be deposited.

Chapter 19: Choosing the Right Insurance Company walks you through the various types of policies and explains the importance of protecting your investment.

PART 7: MOVING

Chapter 20: Moving to the New Home not only offers moving tips and the pros and cons of using a local moving company instead of nationwide movers, but also helps you stay on course before, during and after your relocation with worksheets, checklists and to do lists that you can fill in yourself.

PART 8: NEW TRENDS IN REAL ESTATE

Chapter 21: Is a Nontraditional Home Right for You? focuses on the recent proliferation of home styles, amenities and mortgage options. For example, with the new home communities (where you are the first owner), builders are asking whether you need a "smart house," a "green home" or cable outlets in each room for ubiquitous Internet hook ups. The environmentally friendly homes have top-of-the-line options on doors, windows and heating systems to maximize energy savings and provide the healthiest environment.

PART 9: GRAPH PAPER AND FURNITURE TEMPLATES

And now for the fun part. After all your hard work finding and purchasing your new home, *Home Buying Made Easy* also wants to make sure you get comfortably settled in. To that end, this hands-on section of the book provides miniature furniture templates that you can punch out and move around a graph paper layout of each room in your house. These scaled-down furniture templates let you try out different decorating arrangements without doing any of the heavy lifting.

PART 1:

ARE YOU READY FOR REAL ESTATE?

NOTES

THE OWNERSHIP
ADVANTAGE

The biggest advantage to owning your home can be financial. Homeowner wealth is usually accrued through mortgage payments, which are also seen by many in the industry as "forced savings programs."

Yes, you are paying a great deal of interest, but you are also forced to save a certain amount every month. The further along you get in your mortgage, the less you pay in interest and the more you're paying off the actual cost of the home, or the "principal."

Many retirees achieve a well-earned sense of satisfaction from making their last mortgage payment. At that point, the house is worth many times what they paid for it—considering that, over the last century, home prices have increased an average of 9 to 10 percent each year. Some retirees choose to pay living expenses from their home equity (the money they've paid into their home plus its appreciation) by taking out "reverse mortgages." In exchange for the title of the home, banks pay the retirees a monthly sum. In other words, retirees are finally able to use the money they've saved all those years to pay their daily expenses. They're spending their savings, which they put into their house.

Homeownership is one of the best ways to accrue several hundreds of thousands or even millions of dollars over a lifetime. Owning a home has other advantages that are just as important, even if they are not financial. Homeowners feel reassured about their well-being, knowing that they are building a nest egg. They can also decorate and landscape the house any way they want, thereby expressing their identities. Since homeowners are known as responsible, capable members of society, they get the ego boost when discussing their housing situation with others. Individuals derive great pride and satisfaction from owning a home.

Only those who are convinced they can make such a good return with the same low level of risk via other types of investments should rent a home. Some individuals believe they can and will save and create more wealth if they use their savings and income for other purposes than a mortgage. Entrepreneurs and stock investors may look at the housing decision this way. While it's conceivable that a stock market wiz or business genius can make more money using their cash, most of us cannot claim to be either. In fact, most of them don't turn out to be the great wiz they thought they would be.

RENTING VERSUS OWNING

Take a look at the following table to get a good idea of where renters come out ahead and where buyers get the sweetest deal. It's a good idea to circle or highlight the advantages most important to you. Just like we said in the intro: write all over this book! If you circle more in one column than the other, perhaps that's the best option for you.

	Benefits of Owning	Benefits of Renting
Financial	Part of your monthly mortgage payments go toward building up your equity. You are forced to build up a pool of cash, which you can borrow against in the future. You can write off your interest expense against your income. This is the biggest tax write-off available to Americans. Your mortgage payment remains steady over the years (if you have a fixed rate and don't refinance and use all of the equity). Rents rise, often yearly. You will have more spending money for your retirement years if your house is paid off. In the future (15-20 years), your housing expenses will be lower than someone who rents. Leverage is used most powerfully in real estate than anywhere else in the investment world. For $20,000, a homeowner can (conceivably and given the right conditions) secure a $400,000 investment. That $400,000 could make a 10% gain in two years or less, netting the investor (borrower) $40,000 on their loan, a 200% return.	You don't have to pay for major or minor repairs. You don't have to pay property taxes. You don't have to pay for costs (thousands of dollars) involved in buying and selling a home. Often water, sewer and other utilities are paid by the landlord, not you. You don't have to pay most of the insurance costs. Since you don't have to put all your cash into a down payment, you have more cash to invest in other areas (such as stocks and bonds) or start your own business.
Convenience	You can do almost whatever you want to your home whenever you want to do it. You don't have to depend on a landlord for maintenance and repairs.	You can move on a whim, with a 30-day notice, provided you don't have a long-term lease. It is fairly easy to find a decent rental in a short period of time. You can pick up the phone for a repair. With your landlord responsible for maintaining the property, you don't have to worry about lining up repair people. There's no worry about falling house values.

	Benefits of Owning	Benefits of Renting
Intangibles	Pride in ownership. Status. People who own their own homes are generally viewed as reliable and hard-working. A sense of control over your home decisions. The security that comes from being your own landlord.	Living in close proximity to your neighbors (often sharing common areas such as pools and clubhouses) often provides a built-in social network.
Time Savings	Less time having to move from place to place.	With home repair and renovation, you will spend a fraction of the time researching the home's problem, finding the right repair person and overseeing the job, compared to a homeowner.

GOOD REASONS TO BUY A HOME

A mortgage payment may be higher, even significantly higher, than a rent check in the first ten years or so. Add to that the property taxes, insurance and house maintenance costs, and it can seem ridiculous to own. Over the long term, however, individuals get into trouble renting.

After about ten years, given a modest inflation rate, the benefits of owning a home start accumulating. At that point not only are your monthly payments lower than renting, but you're building up equity more and more quickly. Your house is your bank. As long as you want to live in it, you can keep depositing money into it.

In case of emergencies, your home can lend you the money in the form of tax-deductible, low-interest second mortgages or home equity lines of credit. That said, most homeowners do their best to keep depositing rather than withdrawing.

YOUR HOME AS AN INVESTMENT TOWARD YOUR FUTURE

If you're renting and don't think you can afford the perfect home, why not consider buying a good enough home? It's in your best interest to buy, if you can find a home where your monthly expenses are slightly more than renting. Remember, part of your housing expenses will be going right back to you in the form of home equity. For most Americans, entering the real estate market any way they can is their best bet in eventually getting exactly what they want. Buying even the smallest condominium could be your way out of renting and into homeownership. If you stay long enough for the home to appreciate in price (at least 5 years), you will have that additional equity to put down on a new home. While the first home you can afford may not be in your dream neighborhood, keep reading to see how patience can eventually get you into a home that you will love.

In later chapters, we'll discuss the programs available to get and keep you in your home. While most of the government programs do target lower income families, there are a few for moderate and middle income buyers as well.

If federal and state governments are so determined to get you in a home, they are equally determined to help you stay in that home. There are government mortgage bail out programs, mortgage programs, debt relief programs and down payment procurement programs. If you buy a home, you won't really be shouldering the financial burden all by yourself. Read on to see how you can begin the most financially sound journey of your life.

THE USE OF LEVERAGE

One of the best reasons to invest in real estate is because of the leverage you get on your home value. Say you invest $25,000 in a down payment on a $500,000 home. You would have a loan of $475,000. In one year, if that $500,000 house increases in value by 10 percent, you would have made a $50,000 profit on your $25,000 investment, or a 200 percent profit. On the other hand, say that you take that $25,000 and put it in the bank earning 5 percent interest. In that same time period (one year), you would have made $1,250. So the real estate investment earned you $48,750 more than if you had left the money in your bank. While some years may be up and some down, on the average, real estate appreciates 9 to 10 percent per year. Only in real estate can such a small amount secure such a large investment. Leverage works most effectively in real estate.

BAD REASONS TO BUY A HOME

- You're feeling pressure to buy a home. Don't buy when you're not ready financially or emotionally. Make sure you're committed, or you may fall victim to "buyer's remorse."

- Colleagues and peers are buying and you don't want to be left behind. Instead, wait until the market is right and you have the down payment for what you want.

- It's the time of your life when you should have a house. Don't fret. Just because you don't have a house right now doesn't mean you'll never have one.

- Panic. The market is rising and you want to get into something ... *anything*! Calm your emotions. Markets go up and markets come back down again.

- You think it will resolve some family issues. Remember, even in the new house the old family will be there with you.

THE OWNERSHIP ADVANTAGE

IS REAL ESTATE FOR YOU?

Everyone has their own reasons for wanting to purchase a home. However, not everyone is ready to take this huge step. The following questions will help you decide whether or not you're at a point in your life when purchasing a home would be a smart move.

	Yes	No
1) Is the desire to buy a home yours and no one else's?	☐	☐
2) Are you willing to keep careful track of mortgage statements, property tax statements, insurance forms, etc.?	☐	☐
3) Do you see rent prices in your area rising over the next three years?	☐	☐
4) Is your company stable? Is your job secure? If not, will you be able to find another job easily?	☐	☐
5) Have you examined and built up a good credit history?	☐	☐
6) Do you believe that homeownership is one of the best investments available?	☐	☐
7) When you think of repairing sprinklers and patching up wall gouges, do you have a happy feeling?	☐	☐
8) Do you like going to many stores to find the right drapes, wallpaper, carpets, etc.?	☐	☐
9) Do you expect to stay in your area for more than three years?	☐	☐
10) Do you have several thousand dollars saved up to cover closing costs?	☐	☐
11) After paying your current monthly expenses, do you have extra money? (Costs in owning a home will run a few hundred or even a few thousand dollars more a month than when you are renting)	☐	☐

If you have lots of "no" answers, consider putting your plans on the back burner, but keep this book at the forefront in your library. You can use this time to learn more about real estate, strengthen your credit and save money. If you haven't already, you can also learn to budget. Set some goals as to how much you want to save every month. Whatever you do, don't jump into homeownership without being financially and emotionally ready.

WHY INVEST IN REAL ESTATE?

Before you put all of your money in real estate, think about diversification. Investment experts encourage investors to diversify their investment portfolios. In assets that are listed on paper, investors should have a mix of stocks, bonds and cash instruments (CDs, money market accounts) that's appropriate for their age, financial situation and long-term goals. They must balance the risk they take on with the potential for vigorous returns.

One of your biggest assets is your house. It's not on paper but on land. In fact, at the end of thirty years, you will have an investment of several hundred thousand (if not a million) dollars. Not only do you have to strike a delicate balance among the assets in your investment portfolio, you need to balance those paper assets with your real estate assets.

Experts believe that the skyrocketing home prices in the first five years of the new millennium (2000-2005) were partly attributed to the stock market crash. People pulled their funds out of the market and fast. Not wanting to let the money linger in bank accounts yielding 4-6 percent, they decided to invest in real estate, and homes swelled in price.

As mentioned before, the housing market does not "crash" to the extent that the stock market does. A stock certificate can be sold with a few clicks on the keyboard or a phone call to a broker without changing the owner's day-to-day existence. A home sale is a huge inconvenience both during and after the sale. These factors keep home prices steady.

Watch out for limited real estate partnerships. These investment devices have very high commissions that go to the "financial consultant" or "financial advisor." They also have no qualms about charging annual operating fees of 2 to 3 percent. This is a level much higher than mutual fund annual fees and often higher than the fees of experienced, fee-based financial managers. Limited partnerships are usually not a good deal.

The same goes for commercial real estate investments that seem too good to be true. Avoid any get rich quick scheme that makes outrageous claims about the benefits of investing in commercial real estate. Before you consider investment property, crunch the numbers and see how many years it will take you to break even. It could take years if the mortgage, plus insurance and property taxes add up to more than you can charge for rent. If you want a positive cash flow, then you'll need a big down payment to get the mortgage low enough so that the rent you receive pays for everything, including repairs and maintenance.

NOTES

IS THIS THE RIGHT TIME TO BUY?

The biggest concern on the minds of most people thinking about buying a home is whether or not the conditions are right for buying a home. Would I be foolish to invest now? Will I lose my hard-earned down payment money? If prices have been going up for a few years, there's a risk in buying because the market may be ready for a "correction"—a natural drop in prices of 10 to 20 percent. On the other hand, if you don't buy this year, you run the risk that next year the house of your dreams will cost 15 percent more than it does today. How do you make this fateful decision?

The first piece of information you should reassure yourself with is that, while there are swings in the housing market, the trend has always been and always will be upward. Even during times of war and frightening conflicts around the globe, people still have to buy toilet paper, go to the movies, get shoes for their kids and live in a home. Real estate is a limited quantity—there are only a certain number of houses that come on the market at any one time. Some economists even hold that war is good for the economy. When the government increases its demands on businesses for their goods and services, its dollars stimulate the economy.

This chapter will help you understand the underlying concepts behind economic and housing market swings. You'll find the information to be much more common sense than complex. When you understand the terms behind the trends, you can talk to your real estate agent more intelligently, make better decisions and be confident about those decisions. With hundreds of thousands of dollars at stake, you're smart to educate yourself.

UNDERSTANDING THE HOUSING MARKET

The more homes there are on the market, the lower the price will be. If you see lots of For Sale signs up, you have plenty of options. Realtors refer to this kind of market as "cool" or "soft." Or, they use the classic phrase, "It's a buyer's market." You'll have a better chance at bringing a home price down because the seller knows you can just go down the street to the next house that's for sale. Buyers have more power.

All sellers know this. It's why the next seller may be more motivated to make a deal. You and all the other home buyers out there will be more successful in reducing prices because of the desperation/panic on the seller's side. In response, housing prices will stay low.

If, on the other hand, there are few homes available for sale, Realtors say "inventory is low." The market is "hot" or "tight." It's a seller's market. The sellers have all the power, and the panic/desperation is on the buyer's side. The sellers know people need to get into new houses, whether due to a job change, divorce or any other pressing life circumstance. In these conditions, several desperate buyers may bid on the same house. Some will bid even more than the asking price in order to get the house. Bidding wars like these have occurred in Los Angeles, San Diego, Las Vegas, Miami, Boston and Washington during the first few years of the new millennium. In fact, all of these cities experienced huge percent increases in home prices during this same time period.

In "hot" markets, buyers pay top dollar—or what is considered top dollar for that time period. Nevertheless, it may still be wise to buy a home. If you buy a home during a seller's market, there should not be an immediate financial negative, providing you can wait out any long-term downturn in housing prices.

THE ECONOMIC OUTLOOK

Predicting market trends is a very complicated science. That's why it's important to know the financial and demographic forces at work in the economy. When you have a good grasp of the economy, it's easier to feel confident about your choice to buy property.

There are stable forces in our society today that keep the housing market contained. It's important that you understand them so that you can gauge when the price of your home is going to tumble and when it's going to climb again. Along the way, you will gain the patience and long-range vision of the best and most successful investors.

POPULATION TRENDS

The biggest factor shaping the housing market is population and how it is divided by age and life phase. The three large population groups driving this trend include: the Baby Boomers (78 million strong), followed by Generation X (24 million), and the Baby Boomers' children, known as the New Boomers (71 million and growing). The Baby Boomers (the first born in 1946) began going into apartments in 1971. When they buy and sell dictates the direction of the housing market. They bought their first homes in 1979 and traded up to more expensive homes in 2000.

During the late 1990s the first Baby Boomers (now in their 50s) bought vacation homes, and the middle Baby Boomers (now in their 40s) traded up. At this same time, the youngest Baby Boomers (approaching their 30s) bought their first homes. The market responded to all this demand with skyrocketing housing prices.

Baby Boomers finished trading up by 2005. Since then, the market has been declining. With the stock market declining rapidly during this same period, Baby Boomers looked for a place to put their stock market profits. Real estate proved to be a viable option.

The first Baby Boomers will start to retire in 2008, driving up demand for retirement homes and condos, which will appreciate rapidly in the coming years.

Generation X, defined loosely as those born between 1964 and 1981, is one-third the size of the Baby Boomer group, numbering about 24 million. So far, this group has not driven the housing market to new heights. Generation X started buying their first homes around 1997, but their numbers are so low that they didn't make much of an impact. If you're buying now (which, since you bought this book, you most likely are), don't listen to the media doom and gloom predicting a big fall after an irrational real estate "bubble" or buying frenzy. While the Baby Boomers quietly retire their wallets, you have the Baby Boomers' babies, the New Boomers—also called Generation Y, the Millennium Generation, and the Baby Boom Echo—to lift your home's value into the stratosphere. This generation, currently grade-schoolers, will outpace the Baby Boomers in numbers because of the steady stream of immigrants adding to it. This group, with its first members born in the early 1980s and later ones around the year 2000, will start buying homes in about 2012.

Experts believe the 71 million New Boomers today will eventually surpass the original Baby Boomers in numbers. At that point, we can look forward to a real estate renaissance.

GAUGING THE ECONOMIC HEALTH AND VITALITY OF THE AREA

Besides overall population trends, you can look at other economic forces to help you decide whether you should buy now or wait. Keep in mind the old real estate saying: "the best time to buy real estate is always *ten years ago*." Your *ten years ago* just may be today.

THE JOB MARKET

The more jobs an area has, the more housing it needs. Find out the unemployment rate in your area and whether that number is growing or shrinking. The Bureau of Labor Statistics will have access to these figures. You can also search the online archives of the area's local paper. Use search terms such as "unemployment," "local," and "jobless." A 5 percent unemployment rate is considered low or normal. Areas go into serious recessions when their unemployment rates climb past 10 percent. During recessions, people leave the area to find work elsewhere. They are forced to sell their homes. Driving down any street of an area hit with recession, you'll find several For Sale signs.

After you have an idea about rising or declining unemployment rates, compare it with the national average. Consider whether the downturn in your area is temporary or long-term. You may have to research more to get a longer-range idea of the region's economy.

Numbers can't tell you everything. When researching the job situation in the area where you'll be living, remember to determine what kinds of jobs are growing and what kinds are shrinking. If most of the jobs in a community come from weak employment sectors like farms or small retailers, real estate prices probably won't rise too quickly. The wages in these areas are not high enough to create a whole army of homeowners. Jobs in high growth sectors such as biotechnology and healthcare are high paying. Because people in these fields have home buying in mind, home values in those areas tend to be higher.

AVAILABLE HOMES

Job growth creates a great demand for houses. If there are plenty of houses to go around, housing prices will stay even. In this environment, the city council could be encouraging developers to build more homes than are needed.

Conversely, even in areas with high unemployment, housing prices could be high if no one is building. Low inventory leads to many buyers bidding on the same house, and in our capitalist society, the highest bidder wins. That's a seller's market. It all goes back to "inventory" and the numbers of buyers and sellers. You need to get both sides of the equation: the number of current and potential home buyers *and* the amount of existing and future housing.

Survey your market. Determine if there are a few or many homes out there waiting for you. Remember high inventory gives buyers the power and the upper hand in the market. High inventory gives buyers all the power.

RENTAL VACANCIES

The easiest way to determine the housing supply is to look at the vacancy rates of rentals. This rate is calculated by dividing the number of empty units by the number of total units. So if there are 10,000 rental units in your area and 500 of them are vacant, the vacancy rate is 5 percent, a figure considered to be low. The fewer rental units available, the higher the rents. The higher the rents, the more attractive buying seems. If the vacancy rate is high, say at 7 to 10 percent, landlords are willing to cut rents just to get someone into their units. To find the rate of rental vacancies, go to the online edition of the local newspaper and type in the search terms "rental vacancies," or "housing supply."

BUILDING PERMITS

Looking at the number of building permits issued in an area tells you something about its current real estate climate. This is another way to determine the current and future state of the market. A great number of permits issued means that builders are busy making new homes. When housing prices rise quickly in an area, more building permits are issued.

Look at the trend for at least five years. Keep in mind that many cities limit the amount of new construction. If real estate is limited in the area, there will probably always be a strong demand for housing. In cities like Manhattan, San Francisco, Hawaii, Boston, Hong Kong and Tokyo, they will always have exorbitant real estate prices because you can only build to the water's edge. Where the land stretches as far as you can see on all sides—mostly in the Midwestern regions—home prices rise slowly. You can contact the city's chamber of commerce or the area's building industry association to get the figures on the last few years of building permits issued. The National Association of Home Builders (www.nahb.org) will help you find your local association.

REAL ESTATE RUMORS: TRUE OR FALSE?

Don't be fooled by rumors and hearsay about real estate. Make sure the information that drives you to purchase is backed up by solid facts. For instance, people believe that housing prices are rising in warm areas because retirees are flocking there. According to a 2003 study conducted by the National Association of Home Builders, two-thirds of seniors buying retirement homes are sticking close to their original homes.

LONG-RANGE VISION

Having long-range vision takes some of the uncertainty out of buying a home. Trends like the ones we've discussed have gone on for decades and will continue. We do not pretend to predict the direction of the real estate market in this book. No one can. History tells us that the housing market is not as volatile as the stock market. People are more likely to "wait out" a downturn in their housing value. Be prepared for the media to exaggerate either real estate "crashes" or "explosions." The housing market is far less risky than alarmist media "experts" would lead you to believe.

PART 2:

HOW MUCH HOUSE CAN YOU AFFORD?

NOTES

UNDERSTANDING HOW MUCH YOU CAN AFFORD

You are really worth a great deal. You just don't realize it. Most home buyers call an agent, provide some numbers for their income and savings and wait to be told the very maximum that the bank will allocate for their new home. Rather than going that route, it would be wise to know ahead of time what you can handle financially. The mortgage lender doesn't factor in your children's college fund or your own retirement goals. You need to have a good picture of how much you can afford as well as how much you want to spend.

Compare your loan figures with the bank's and Realtor's numbers. It could be that they quote too little or too much. Either way, knowing the terms involved will give you the power to make an informed and confident decision. It will also encourage Realtors and mortgage experts to take you seriously. Arm yourself with as much information as possible. With your own figures in front of you from the very beginning, you are the one in control.

Keep in mind that few people take a loan for less than what the bank tells them they can afford. Perhaps you should be an exception to that trend. As exciting as a huge loan amount sounds, it could be a budgeting nightmare in the making. Stretching your finances to the limit in order to pay back all that money can prove uncomfortable at best and impossible at worst.

YOUR HOUSING EXPENSE RATIO

The mortgage lender makes a loan decision on a non-personal basis. He or she decides how much they're willing to lend you based on two types of information: your income versus expenses, and your credit report. The lender's primary motivation is to take on an acceptable risk for a profit. Lending institutions have formulas and thresholds that help them determine whether or not you're trustworthy.

Lenders have determined that a typical family's monthly housing expenses (*Principal + Interest + Taxes + Insurance*) should equal no more than 28 percent of its gross monthly income before taxes.

Lenders consider this sum, abbreviated as PITI, to be your housing expense. Your housing expense ratio is your housing expense divided by your gross monthly income. Lenders strive to keep that ratio at no higher than 28 percent.

Being judged as a whole by the housing expense ratio is not technically fair. A frugal homeowner could get away with spending 35 percent of their income on housing. The bank assumes that you have certain expenses that you might not have. If you don't put income into fancy cars and clothes, more of your cash could conceivably go to your house. You would be punished for the big-spending homeowner who has high car payments and department store balances. With such fine tastes, these types of homeowners need to be restricted to what they can really afford. In other words, the bank is most likely to make the most money overall when it keeps the housing expense ratio at 28 percent, as an average for most buyers.

The Federal Housing Administration helped determine that number through studies conducted in the 1930s and 1940s, and they've stuck with it ever since. Over the years, 28 percent of gross monthly income has proven to be the most reliable gauge for the mortgage industry.

To figure the maximum mortgage payment the bank is going to say you can afford, simply multiply your gross monthly income by .28 (gross income x .28). The following table applies that formula to some sample incomes.

Gross Monthly Income	Housing Expense Ratio	Maximum Monthly Mortgage Payment (PITI)
$3,000	.28	$840
$3,500	.28	$980
$4,000	.28	$1,120
$5,000	.28	$1,400
$6,000	.28	$1,680
$7,000	.28	$1,960

How accurate is 28 percent of gross monthly income? It's based on the bank's estimation and the default habits of the average consumer. This doesn't necessarily reflect your personal financial habits. The bank's assumption is that you need the remaining 72 percent of your income to cover income taxes, medical bills, clothing, car payments, food and school expenses. If you spend less than the average person, they will approve you for less than what you could afford. Alas, the world is not fair. You will not get the bank to budge from their preset thresholds.

If you're a big spender and the bank approves you for more money than you expected, you might have a hard time making your payments. Leave a little wiggle room to spend on the things you like. Otherwise, you'll be pouring it into your one big purchase—the home itself—and quickly resent it for cramping your style.

WARNING! Don't be tempted to fudge your income on the tax returns you give the lender. The self-employed have the greatest opportunity to do this. Now more than ever, income exaggerators get caught. When you're ready to close your loan, lenders often ask you to sign a form authorizing them to request a copy of your income tax return from the IRS.

Getting caught inflating your income can be more than just embarrassing. Buying a house beyond one's means can cause enormous stress. People ruin their health, relationships and happiness worrying about making mortgage payments. It could also limit freedom to build up enough savings to switch jobs, allow a parent to stay home with a child or move as needed. The decision to buy a home and acquire a loan can affect homeowners for decades, if not the rest of their lives. Because financial issues can cause stress, many people avoid tallying their assets and liabilities. If you want to buy a house, you need a crystal clear picture of your finances.

ASSETS AND LIABILITY WORKSHEET

This worksheet compares what you have with what you owe. Fill in the current balance for each of the items listed and then total them up. The information you provide here will not only help you prepare for the lenders, but also give you a concrete idea of where you stand and what kind of budget you have to work with.

YOUR ASSETS

Bank Accounts

Checking:
Savings:

Investments

Real Estate:
Stocks:
Bonds:
Mutual Funds:

Retirement

IRA:
401(k):
403(b):

Total Assets: $

YOUR LIABILITIES

Loans

Student:
Car:
Mortgage:

Credit Cards

MasterCard:
Visa:
American Express:
Other Credit Cards:

Other Debt

:
:

Total Liabilities: $

YOUR OVERALL DEBT RATIO

The housing expense ratio is not the only formula lenders use to determine your debt worthiness. To qualify for a loan, lenders also require that all of your monthly expenses, both housing expenses (PITI) and recurring payments, total no more than 36 percent of your gross monthly income. Rest assured that lenders do not consider living expenses such as gas, electric, cable and telephone bills to be debt. The debt they focus on for this formula is larger sums of money that you've actually borrowed. In other words, it's "debt outstanding" or "recurring debt" on which you make regular, consistent payments. This debt includes car loans, student loans and credit card balances. This figure, known as the overall debt ratio, gives lenders more information about your spending habits. Lenders use this figure to determine how much to lend.

You can determine your overall debt ratio by following the steps below:

Step 1: Multiply your Gross Monthly Income by 36 percent.

Step 2: Add up all of your monthly recurring payments:

Car payment	$_____
Student loan payment	$_____
Credit card payment	$_____
Other loans	$_____
Other recurring payments	$_____
Total Recurring Payments	$_____

Step 3: Figure out your PITI (monthly payment including principal, interest, homeowner's insurance and property taxes). To figure the PI (principal and interest payment), use the mortgage calculator on page 79. Then, add your monthly homeowner's insurance (call your insurance agent for an estimate) and property taxes (use 2 percent of the sale price as a guess or ask a real estate agent for a more accurate number).

Step 4: Find your Total Monthly Expenses by adding the PITI on your future home with the Total Recurring Payments.

Step 5: You will qualify for the loan if 36 percent of your Gross Monthly Income is equal to or greater than your Total Monthly Expenses.

For Example: Lets say your gross annual income is $75,000. 36 percent of your Gross Monthly Income is (75,000 ÷ 12) x (.36) = $2,250. Lets say that you have a $125 monthly car payment, a $75 monthly credit card payment, and a $100 monthly student loan payment. Your total Recurring Monthly Payments are $300. Let's say your PITI is $1400. Add your PITI with your Recurring Monthly Payments to get your Total Monthly Expenses ($1,400 + $300 = $1,700). Since 36% of your Gross Monthly Income is $2,250 and your total monthly expenses is $1,700 you would qualify for the loan.

Fill in the blank spaces below to calculate your chances of getting your loan approved (use the mortgage payment calculator on page 79 to determine your PI):

.36 x _____   must be   _____
         Gross Monthly Income   greater than   Total Monthly Expenses
                                                or equal to

TRACKING YOUR INCOME AND EXPENSES

One of the first steps toward any financial goal is to establish a budget. To get a general idea of what you are spending and saving, follow these steps:

Step 1: Label file folders or manila envelopes with common headings such as Taxes, Housing, Retirement, Savings, Transportation, Food, Clothing, Debt Payments, Entertainment, Professional Advice, Health Care, Insurance, Child-Related Expenses and Charity.

Step 2: Keep these files in a convenient place, such as a file cabinet or small accordion file. Every time you have a receipt, place it in the correct slot. After you pay bills, put the stubs in the files. If you pay your bills online, jot down how much and when you paid each creditor. If you use credit cards, review your monthly statements and jot down how much money went to each category.

Step 3: In the meantime, begin filling out the "Income" portion of the *Income and Expense Worksheet*. (You might want to consider making a few copies of the blank tables first.)

Step 4: When the next month's bills arrive, don't put them in the files right away. Instead, bind the papers, stubs and notes for the first month with a rubber band or binder clip.

Step 5: Add up the expenses and enter them in the *Income and Expense Worksheet*.

Try to be as honest and forthcoming as possible when filling out these tables. If you're not, you'll only have financial stress down the road. The purpose of these tables is twofold: to get a clear picture of what you can afford and to give the bank a clear picture of what you can afford. Of course, the bank is just going to stick to 28 percent or 36 percent of your gross income, whichever is lower, in determining your loan amount.

The following five worksheets will help you determine your income/expense ratio. After keeping track of your expenses for a month, enter the amounts for each category under the "Current" column. These worksheets also allow you to estimate what your expenses will run after you purchase the house, and three to five years down the road.

Monthly Income:

Income	Current	After House Purchase	In 3-5 years
From Primary Job			
From Second Job			
From Dividends and Interest			
From Expected Capital Gains			
From Child Support or Alimony			
Other			
Total Monthly Income			

Monthly Expenses:

Expense	Current	After House Purchase	In 3-5 years
Taxes			
Social Security			
Federal			
State and Local			
Other			
Total Taxes			
Housing			
Mortgage Payment			
Homeowner's Insurance			
Property Taxes			
Private Mortgage Insurance (PMI)			
Maintenance/Repairs			
Total Housing			

Expense	Current	After House Purchase	In 3-5 years
Utilities			
Gas			
Electric			
Water/Sewer			
Total Utilities			
Miscellaneous			
Pet Care & Boarding			
Cleaning Services			
Telephone			
Cell Phone			
Other			
Total Miscellaneous			
Transportation			
Car/Lease Payment(s)			
Auto Repairs			
Auto Maintenance			
Gasoline			
Parking			
Tolls			
Public Transportation			
Taxis			
Other			
Total Transportation			
Retirement/Savings			
IRA/401(k)			
Stock/Bond Investments			
Emergency Fund			
Personal Savings			
College Fund			
Down Payment Fund			
Travel/Vacation Savings			
Christmas Savings			
Other			
Total Retirement/Savings			

Expense	Current	After House Purchase	In 3-5 years
Food			
Groceries			
Restaurants			
Snacks			
Other			
Total Food			
Debt Payments			
Credit Cards			
Auto Loans			
Student Loans			
Other			
Total Debt Payments			
Health Care			
Health Insurance			
Medical/Dental Co-pays			
Medication			
Vitamins			
Therapy			
Health Club/Gym			
Other			
Total Health Care			
Entertainment			
Movies			
Hobbies			
Theater/Concerts			
Magazines/Newspapers			
CDs/Videos			
Cable/Satellite TV			
Internet			
Vacation			
Gifts			
Other			
Total Entertainment			

Expense	Current	After House Purchase	In 3-5 years
Clothing/Apparel			
Partner 1			
Partner 2			
Child 1			
Child 2			
Child 3			
Child 4			
Total Clothing/Apparel			
Shoes			
Partner 1			
Partner 2			
Child 1			
Child 2			
Child 3			
Child 4			
Jewelry			
Total Shoes			
Personal Care			
Dry Cleaning			
Haircuts			
Makeup			
Total Personal Care			
Professional Advice			
Accountant			
Attorney			
Financial Planner			
Other			
Total Professional Advice			

Expense	Current	After House Purchase	In 3-5 years
Other Insurance			
Disability			
Life			
Long-Term Care			
Other			
Total Other Insurance			
Child-Related			
Private School Tuition			
Private School Fees			
Teacher Gifts			
Field Trips			
Books			
Supplies			
Day Care			
Babysitter			
Toys			
Child Support			
Other			
Total Child-Related			
Charity			
Church			
Other			
Total Charity			
Total Monthly Expenses			

NOTES

YOUR CREDIT REPORT

Whether or not you get approved for a home loan depends on your FICO score. In the credit world, FICO is the most widely known credit scoring system. It stands for Fair Isaac Corporation and is used by Experian, TransUnion and Equifax, the top three credit bureaus in the United States. When you apply for a loan, the credit bureaus evaluate your credit profile and assign a score. The score is used to estimate your credit standing. Your FICO score shows lenders how responsible (or irresponsible) you've been when borrowing money in the past.

WHAT CREDIT SCORE DO I NEED FOR A HOME LOAN?

FICO evaluates credit reports and assigns a score between 300 and 800. If you have a FICO score of 660 points or higher, you'll qualify for the best financing. A score between 620 and 660 means you'll be writing letters explaining why you didn't make a particular car payment right on the first of the month.

FICO scores are determined by the following elements:

• Timely repayment of debt. Points are taken off for slow or no payments.

• Past payment history (counts for about 35 percent of the score). The fewer late payments, the better off you'll be.

• Foreclosures/bankruptcies. Big points off for these.

• Credit history (counts for about 15 percent of the score). Longevity counts in your favor. The longer the accounts have been open, the better your credit score will be. Opening new accounts and closing seasoned accounts can bring down the score considerably.

• Types of credit used (counts for about 10 percent of the score). Financing accounts score lower than bank or department store accounts.

- Inquiries about your score (counts for about 10 percent of the score). It looks fishy if you've applied for more than three cards in the last six months.

- Amount you currently owe (counts for about 30 percent of the score). It's best if you only owe 50 percent or less of your credit limit on each card.

- How long you've had the credit cards (counts for about 15 percent of the score). The longer, the better. Having a card for 10 years or longer looks very good.

- Your money management. If you borrowed more than you could ever pay off in a reasonable time, points are taken off. Points are awarded if you have a good balance of credit cards (revolving loans) and car or student loans (installment loans).

You may be considered a higher credit risk or a "sub prime" borrower if you've made late and/or slow payments on housing debt (either your current mortgage payment or your rent), installment credit (a car loan or an appliance like a refrigerator from Sears) or revolving credit (Visa, MasterCard or department store credit cards).

Many of us have made late payments and missed payments. If banks lent money only to those with perfect credit, they'd be desperate for business. You will still get a loan if you have some late or slow payments on your credit report, but you may not get the best rate or deals. Take a look at your credit report before you call a real estate agent and certainly before you call a lender. Don't leave it up to them to report your credit rating.

Use the following form to keep track of your credit report and credit standing. You can also record any questions you have.

Date you ordered the credit report: _____

Your credit score: _____

Inconsistencies: _____

_____

_____

Discrepancies: _____

_____

_____

Errors: _____

_____

_____

Federal law requires that you have access to any information in your credit files and that you are entitled to one free credit report each year. The three biggest credit bureaus include:

Equifax
1-800-685-1111
www.equifax.com

Experian
1-888-397-3742
www.experian.com

TransUnion
1-800-888-4213
www.transunion.com

IMPROVING YOUR CREDIT REPORT

If you have only a few late payments, you'll probably be able to explain them. Late mortgage payments often occur when homeowners move and bills are slowed down with the change-of-address system. If you recently divorced, bills may have gotten into the wrong mailbox and/or lost. Once you understand the cause for the late payment, an explanatory letter to the lender can make all the difference.

If, on the other hand, you're shocked at the results of your credit report, you can turn to a personal credit counseling organization for help. These professionals can help you find ways to improve your credit score. You'll find out that late payments are almost as bad as no payments.

After looking over your credit report, credit counselors can tell you what you can do to raise your score. With their help, creditors often waive late and over limit fees.

Bad debt stays on your credit record for seven years. After that, it's dropped from your record. If you file for bankruptcy, that information stays on your record for ten years. But most lenders only look at your track record for the last two years.

WARNING! Watch out for any services promising to clean up your credit report. Your credit history is just that—a history—and as such it can't be magically wiped clean. If there are mistakes or discrepancies in your credit report, you can correct those yourself.

FIXING YOUR CREDIT REPORT

Sometimes a creditor or even the credit report agency makes a mistake. If that is the case, ask your mortgage lender to get a representative from a credit bureau to help you correct it. Before you apply for a loan, it's best to know ahead of time what your credit rating is and if there are errors on the credit report that need to be corrected.

Once the mistake is corrected with one credit agency, it is your responsibility to call each of the other two to clear it with them as well. If you write in, be sure to include your name and address for the past five years, as well as your Social Security number, date of birth, current employer, phone number and signature. Delineate the problem and add any letters or documentation from any of the other credit bureaus that already corrected the error.

STRENGTHENING YOUR CREDIT

Some frugal people keep very few or no credit cards. While this may be a great device to prevent spending, it doesn't help you when you want to buy a house. You need to establish a track record of incurring debt and clearing it in a timely manner. Open a couple of credit cards in your name. Make sure you have a bank account with your name as the primary account holder. Work to build positive credit references by paying bills on time.

LOWERING CREDIT CARD DEBT

While you have probably heard this before, the quickest way to lower your monthly credit card bill is to switch to a card with a lower interest rate. If you haven't received any good offers in the mail recently, go to www.bankrate.com to shop for a rate that could be lower than your existing rate with no transfer fee. Make sure you maintain enough savings to keep your family afloat for three months in case of an emergency.

If you have many credit cards with significant debt, work on paying them off one by one. Another trick is to cut up all your credit cards and use only a debit card (also called a check card). This takes the money from your account as you spend it, a move that's sure to rein in your spending habits.

If you have savings, use it to pay down the debt. Your house will turn into your savings bank. A balance of $10,000 in savings that's earning 5 percent means you're making $500 per year. If you have $10,000 in credit card debt with a 19 percent annual percentage rate, you're paying $1,900 over the same year. In other words, you're paying $1,400 just to keep your $10,000 in a savings account! You're losing 14 percent on your money, and it's not helping you in the long run.

If you already own your home, explore a home equity line of credit to pay down high interest debts. While this will reduce the amount of your down payment for your next house, it is better than paying 13 to 19 percent on credit card debt. Plus, you can write off interest expense on a home equity line of credit, a move which further brings down the interest rate.

INFORMATION YOUR LENDER WILL REQUIRE

It is very important to file all items needed for the lender, including paycheck stubs and income information from your current job; tax returns for the past two years; alimony and/or child support documents; and any investment documents.

When you meet with your lender, you will probably be asked a long list of questions about your financial history. Here are some sample questions that you should be ready to answer.

- What is the amount of your down payment?
- What is the source of this money? Is it split between you and someone else?
- Specify this arrangement. What is the percentage you are contributing?
- How much is from another source?
- Will there be enough funds to cover closing costs?
- What is your monthly income before subtracting taxes?
- Do you have an existing mortgage? If so, what is your monthly payment?
- How much debt do you have?
- Do you pay rent? If so, what is the monthly amount?
- How long have you been employed at your present job?
- Have you received any employee bonuses over the past two years? If so, what are they?
- Are you self-employed? If so, what is your monthly income?
- Do you pay alimony or child support? If so, what is the amount?
- Do you think there will be any issues of concern on your credit report? If so, can you explain any discrepancies, inconsistencies or errors?

DOCUMENTS REQUIRED FOR LOAN PREAPPROVAL WORKSHEET

This worksheet allows you to track down all the paperwork you will need for loan preapproval. You can record what you have and what you still need.

Item	Found and Filed
Proof of Identity	
Birth Certificate	
Addresses for past 2 years	
Income	
Paycheck Stubs	
Job History	
W-2s for the past 2 years	
Other income: rental properties, family trust fund, stocks, and/or retirement accounts	
Part-time Business	
If self-employed, also include copy of tax returns for 2 years	
If self-employed, also include profit and loss statement	
Loan	
Mortgage	
Trust Deed	
Payment Statements	
Satisfaction of Mortgage	
Reconveyance Deed	
Finances	
Banks (names, addresses and contact info)	
Bank Statements (3 most recent)	
Brokerage Statements (3 most recent)	
Copy of Gift Letter (if funds are coming from elsewhere)	
Copies of Tax Returns for past 2 years	
Current Balance Sheet (if self-employed)	
Year-to-Date Profit and Loss Statement (if self-employed)	
Proof of Bonuses	
Letter of Explanation for Credit Delinquency	
Debt Information (names, addresses, account numbers and balances)	
Cars (make, model, year and current value)	
Other	
Any letters you have written to credit card companies to resolve negative credit history	

THE DOWN PAYMENT

Most lenders are looking for a down payment between 10 and 20 percent of the purchase price of a home. Lenders have learned over the years that homeowners are more reluctant to let a home go into foreclosure when they have made a down payment that large. Banks are far less likely to lose money on a property when there is a 20 percent down payment.

If you don't have a 20 percent down payment, you can still qualify for a loan. The trend is going toward lower down payments. House prices are so high that a 20 percent down payment can be close to $100,000 in some areas. Most consumers haven't saved that much in cash. To keep issuing loans, banks have to find customers where they can. With a down payment of less than 20 percent, you will most likely have to pay for private mortgage insurance (PMI), which can run you up to $100 each month. Private mortgage insurance protects the lender if you default. Once your equity reaches 20 percent, you will be allowed to cancel your private mortgage insurance policy. To remove the PMI, your lender is likely to insist that an appraisal be done and that you pay for that appraisal. Because this is standard practice, there is not much you can do about it.

Loans with less than a 20 percent down payment incur higher closing costs and a higher interest rate on the mortgage. The lender considers them a higher risk and charges these clients more for the privilege of borrowing money. These costs may be negligible if housing prices continue to rise in your area and you let another year pass before buying.

SAVING FOR A DOWN PAYMENT

This is the best strategy for a housing market in which prices are staying flat or even declining. Try to trim your expenses and stick to a tight budget for a while. Consider getting a roommate or renting out a spare room (if your area's CC&Rs or your landlord allow it). The more you save each month, the faster you will realize your goal.

THE DOWN PAYMENT

BORROWING FROM RETIREMENT ACCOUNTS

Some employer retirement plans allow you to borrow against your account in order to make a home down payment. Other plans even let you make outright withdrawals for a first-time home purchase without incurring penalties. Ask your accountant whether you will be liable for taxes owed on that sum of money and put money aside to pay them. Check into the terms of your IRA to see how that sum of money can help you get into a house.

Consider money in your retirement account as your source of last resort. IRAs have tax savings advantages you can't get anywhere else. Your employer may be matching your contributions to the IRA account. The earlier you start saving for retirement, the better. Time multiplies your money like nothing else.

ASKING FAMILY MEMBERS

Chances are your parents, grandparents, aunts and uncles received family assistance at some point in their lifetime. Perhaps they are now in a position to help you out a little bit. Usually parents find it very satisfying to help their children acquire a better standard of living than they themselves enjoyed. More than 20 percent of all first-time home buyers receive assistance from relatives.

Each year, people are allowed to "gift" $10,000 to anyone tax-free. Any sum or merchandise valued over $10,000 is subject to a gift tax. Depending on your circumstances, this can be quite high. If it's November and you're going to need $20,000 by spring, a relative could give you $10,000 before the current year is out and another $10,000 when the new year starts. If they're willing to do so, relatives could also help you reduce student or car loans. This would lower your overall debt ratio so you could qualify for a higher mortgage.

FEDERAL GOVERNMENT RESOURCES

The Federal Housing Administration (FHA), a part of the U.S. Department of Housing and Urban Development (HUD), insures loans for those who can only make a down payment of less than 3 percent. Note that it only *insures* loans; it doesn't *provide* loans. The FHA guarantees a loan you get from a traditional mortgage lender. You find an FHA loan through traditional lenders. The bank is willing to lend you the money because if you do default, the government will pay it back.

Private mortgage insurance on FHA loans can run up to 3.8 percent of the loan amount. The FHA has twice the rate of delinquent payments compared to a traditional mortgage broker. You can add the one-time 3.8 percent to the mortgage amount. After the first 3.8 percent payment, you will be expected to pay a fee of .5 percent of the loan amount each year as well.

The FHA is the only government agency that is entirely self-sufficient. It costs taxpayers nothing, earning all of its income from its mortgage insurance paid by the homeowners. Beyond that, the FHA stimulates the economy by boosting the sales of homes and home-related products (dishwashers, carpeting, lawn supplies), which translates into jobs, more taxes and more businesses.

If you have served in the United States armed forces, you can qualify for a loan from Veterans Affairs (formerly the Veteran's Administration). With a VA loan, you don't have to make any down payment, and you can get an interest rate lower than what your non-uniformed neighbors pay. Widows and widowers of veterans all qualify. Like the FHA, the VA doesn't lend its own money; it simply guarantees to pay the money if the homeowner defaults on the loan.

STATE GOVERNMENT RESOURCES

If you are a low- or moderate-income home buyer, there are special programs designed to help you. These loans are available through private lenders, as well as local and state housing agencies like the California Housing Finance Agency (CalHFA). Most lenders specializing in real estate mortgage loans are aware of these types of loan programs. In Minnesota, they work with the Minnesota Housing Finance Agency. In Kentucky, the Kentucky Housing Corporation provides low-cost loan programs. There are income ceilings involved with all of these loan programs, but you may qualify depending on your income.

LOCAL GOVERNMENT RESOURCES

In every city, there's an office that covers affordable housing—such as the Seattle Office of Housing, the San Diego Housing Commission and the Housing Authority of the City of Pittsburgh. In addition to pointing you in the direction of affordable loans and perhaps even guaranteeing the loans, they might have home improvement grants (free money) available as well. Some offices offer second mortgages and even grants for down payments.

Consider these resources before you consign yourself to a lifetime of renting. Keep in mind that the federal, state and local governments all want you to be a homeowner. The correlation between homeownership and good citizenship has been proven in study after study. It's in the government's best interest that you own a home. Let them help you.

THE DOWN PAYMENT

WARNING! In slow markets, a desperate builder may offer a "no down payment" or "zero down payment" mortgage program. Use caution here. The lender will make up for the bargain with high closing costs and a high interest rate. You will also have to pay private mortgage insurance.

REAL ESTATE PARTNERSHIPS

There are several scenarios in which it could be wise to pull another party into your real estate purchase. For instance, if your parents are reluctant to lend you the money for a home down payment, they might go for a "shared equity" deal instead. In this arrangement, the person with the money (called the owner-investor) pays the down payment and the closing costs. The occupant (called the owner-occupant) lives in the home and pays the monthly mortgage, the property taxes and the maintenance. At the end of a certain time—often five years—the house is sold, and either the two owners split the profit, or the owner-occupant borrows against the appreciation of the house and pays off the owner-investor. At this time, the owner-occupant can refinance the loan with only his or her name on the deed.

An accountant or attorney can draw up the documents needed in an arrangement like this. Get everything in writing. Strict documentation is a necessity, as with all legal matters.

Another shared equity situation exists when two owners go in together on a home or a duplex that contains two separate apartments. Again, make sure to have everything in writing. When money is involved, emotions are not far behind. Make sure your documentation includes:

• Title ownership by all parties
• The share of property owned by each buyer
• A buyout clause if one of you wants to sell
• How the profits will be divided
• Method for resolving disputes (possibly through mediation)
• Whether any capital improvements will be permitted and how payment will be handled
• Division of any maintenance costs

You may find that your mortgage lender dislikes your equity-sharing plan. It may insist that only the owner-occupant's income be considered when determining the amount of a loan. Don't be surprised if you are quoted a higher interest rate and higher fees than you would have been quoted on your own.

Use the following two worksheets to keep track of the various ways you can increase your down payment. Fill in the sections that apply to your situation. Keep in mind that most lenders prefer a down payment that's 10 to 20 percent of the home's purchase price.

Source	Contact Info	Date Contacted	Result	Date Received	Amount
Assets					
Retirement Account					
Forgotten Assets					
Assistance from Family/Friend					
Seller Financing					

Source	Contact Info	Date Contacted	Result	Date Received	Amount
Federal Government Program					
State Government Program					
Local Government Program					
Real Estate Partnership					
				TOTAL :	

PART 3:

ALL ABOUT FINANCING

PART 3: ALL ABOUT FINANCING

UNDERSTANDING THE MORTGAGE PROCESS

Up until the 1970s, almost every home buyer acquired a 30-year fixed rate loan. As the types of American families began to change drastically, so too did the mortgage industry. The 30-year home loan has fractured into hundreds of different types of loans, many with strange-sounding names like "piggyback," "hybrid" or even "balloon."

With so many types of loans available, the lending landscape is like a smorgasbord. You can choose from the buffet of options and find a loan that works for your financial and family situations.

Some home buyers may need to get in on a reasonable market before prices start going up. Yet their salary is not quite what it will be in five years. For those people, a hybrid loan that has a lower initial fixed rate for the first five years and then switches to an adjustable rate after that period could be the best option.

Others who are concerned about the volatility of future rates might want to lock in a reasonable fixed rate at the beginning and coast through the next 30 years, confident that their payment will never change. In a third scenario, the housing market may be so slow that a clever investor cannot resist buying a fixer-upper. If the teaser rate on an adjustable rate mortgage is set at 4.5 percent for one year, the investor stands to make good money doing some repairs and renting the home for a year or two. When the market regains some strength, the investor can consider reselling the home for a tidy profit without having paid too much in interest expenses.

With a little research on your part, you can find the loan instruments that most closely meet your needs. A mortgage lender will probably tell you the highest monthly payment that he thinks you are most likely to pay consistently without defaulting. This does not take into consideration things like the $200 you want to put into a retirement account each month or the $300 you stash away for your children's college education. Lenders want to charge you for the most money their risk tolerance will allow. Consider your other goals when the lender presents a mortgage figure. Will you have enough left over for these other priorities? Mortgage bankers report that borrowers rarely choose to borrow less than the bank will approve. Be the exception if you dare and if your situation calls for it.

UNDERSTANDING THE MORTGAGE PROCESS

While your agent may recommend a mortgage lender, be cautious. The agent may have fallen into a comfortable relationship with the mortgage lender. Your agent may not have compared that lender's rates and products against any others recently. Remember, real estate agents are not mortgage specialists. They do not have the time and energy to be searching for the best rates. That job is left up to a mortgage broker.

Listen to what your agent has to say about a lender, but shop around yourself. If your time is limited, contact a mortgage broker.

THE ROLE OF THE MORTGAGE BROKER

Despite what you may think, a mortgage broker will not end up costing you more than if you had gone directly to a bank yourself. The bank pays the mortgage broker out of its own costs and fees. They view the mortgage broker as an independent agent—a kind of freelance employee—of their organization. If you go directly to the bank, it will spend time and money using its own personnel to gather your information and documents. The bank is fine with paying an outside agent to do this for them. Your costs are not increased if you use the mortgage broker middleman.

Before a bank or a mortgage broker tells you what their rates are, it's best to understand what the rates are like in your market. Otherwise, it might be hard to know if you're getting a good deal or not. Shopping around is key. If you know the rates firsthand, you will have more confidence and feel more in control when you speak to a lender or broker.

When contacting mortgage brokers, make sure to ask them how many lenders they deal with and how they keep up with the newest lenders and loans in the market. Since you have taken the time to read this book and become familiar with mortgage types and terms, you'll be able to ask the broker informed questions. If the broker seems shaky on the details of each loan, be cautious. Be equally cautious if the broker doesn't seem motivated to explain the loan's important features. Keep in mind that most people contacting mortgage brokers don't know an adjustable rate mortgage from a fixed rate mortgage. The broker is used to working with people who take them at their word. In the best case scenario, the broker will appreciate your competence and work to find you the best loan. If the broker seems taken aback or perturbed by your knowledge or questioning, there are thousands of other brokers out there who can find you a good rate.

HOW THE BORROWING PROCESS WORKS

Home buyers often think banks are doing them a big favor by lending them money to buy a house. In reality, the situation is just the opposite. Banks are basically selling the use of their cash. While their cash goes off their balance sheets, your home goes right onto it. Often a home is a better asset to have on a balance sheet than cash. It certainly appreciates faster. Granted, your home is only on their balance sheet in the form of a loan. But they are getting more money for that loan than they would get in equally safe investments such as treasury bonds or certificates of deposit.

A bank is merely a vendor that sells money for a fee. You are *not* beholden to them. They will give you their money if you pay them interest. In turn, they invest the interest free and clear. In the meantime, you are basically investing their $200,000 or $300,000 or $500,000 into your own home. The bank usually borrows money against that asset, earning them even more money than the interest you pay them. You might have noticed that some mortgage lender commercials now attest that banks should be competing for your business. Indeed, they should be courting you, bringing flowers, chocolates, low rates, competitive costs and respectful interchange. Let them fight for you.

HOW YOUR MORTGAGE RATE IS DETERMINED

A big part of understanding a mortgage is learning how much various banks, credit unions, the federal government and other financial institutions charge each other for using money. Each of these entities lends money to others, from businesses to consumers to overseas businesses and governments. They pass money and assets around, trying to sell (or lend) money for more than they pay to buy (borrow) it. If they can sell money for a point or two higher than what they pay to bring it in, they make a profit.

At the top of this food chain is the United States Federal Reserve System (often called the "Fed"), a government-associated body. It sets the basic rates for banks, car dealerships, loan companies, credit unions, etc. The Fed aims to keep the best balance between recession and inflation, both economy killers that eventually lead to higher unemployment. As a nonpartisan entity, it acts in the best interests of the overall economy, not in the interests of the current administration.

The Federal Reserve System sets the "federal funds rate," the rate that member banks charge each other for overnight loans that banks keep with the Federal Reserve. It also directly sets the discount rate, which is the interest rate that banks pay the Fed to borrow directly from it. Both of these rates influence the "Wall Street Journal prime rate," which tends to be 3 percent points higher than the federal funds rate. The prime rate is the basis on which most banks set their loans for their best customers.

Interest rates drive the economy. When the Federal Reserve lowers interest rates, economic activity picks up because the cost of borrowing money is lower. This makes it easier for consumers and businesses to get inexpensive dollars to buy and build new homes and businesses. Both types of spenders make enough money that the interest charges are worth it. Conversely, when the Fed raises interest rates and money gets too expensive to borrow, people borrow less and spend less.

Why would the Fed raise rates to slow down spending? Spending is good, but only to a point. If consumers have a lot of cash in their pockets, vendors raise prices. Some types of goods are limited in quantity, so the only consumers who get to acquire them are those who pay the most.

When the Federal Reserve raises interest rates, the economy slows. The Fed usually adjusts the federal funds rate by .25 percent or .50 percent at a time over a period of years. The nightly news often discusses the "direction" of these rates. If the Federal Reserve seems to be in a mood to loosen or lower interest rates for a while, an adjustable rate mortgage could make the most sense for you. If, on the other hand, the Federal Reserve is in the mood to "tighten" or raise interest rates, it's best to get the lowest fixed rate loan you can before the rates climb.

Before you jump into a loan, take a look at the greater economic forces that direct interest rates. Understand the mortgage terminology your lender or broker sends your way. Ask your lender or broker questions about anything that is unclear. You'll feel more confident and in control when you understand their explanations and are able to use that knowledge in making your loan decision.

LOAN CONSIDERATIONS BASED ON LIFE STAGES

If you go with the law of averages, you will buy your first home at 33, trade up at 44, buy a vacation home at 52 and buy a retirement home at 65. At all of these stages, different financial pressures and rewards exist. Finding the right mortgage for your situation will factor into the balance of your stress and happiness for a long time to come.

Considerations for Singles

With only one income, it's often hard to come up with a substantial down payment. However, lenders are becoming more and more flexible and particularly amenable to those with limited funds. The prevalence of 100 percent mortgage financing signals the shift in attitude. Before the turn of the millennium, lenders considered these products too risky for themselves and consumers. Because 100 percent financing was offered only by lenders with the highest interest rates, established lenders regarded it as a type of scam.

Now, even the biggest institutions regard 100 percent financing as a practical option. With no down payment required, the biggest barrier to buying a home falls by the wayside. In fact, many singles buy condominiums or townhomes to get started down the property-owning path. A two-bedroom condo often sells for 20 percent to 30 percent less than a two-bedroom detached home with the same square footage. Your overall maintenance and repair expenses will be lower as well, because you're sharing the costs with many other owners. Condominiums usually come with amenities like pools, tennis courts and exercise rooms. Since you're not in the "nesting" stage yet, you probably won't be in the mood to spend a lot of money renovating the condominium. The money you save can go toward a down payment on a larger house.

Before you sign off on this mortgage, consider your next one. How long do you think you will be in this first home? If you're thinking of a short time frame—say three to five years—pay as few points as you can. It will be more worthwhile to pay a .35 percent higher interest rate to save your cash up front. Invest it in something safe so that your money will grow into a decent down payment for your next house. Those with a short time frame should seriously consider an adjustable rate mortgage. An adjustable with a teaser rate lasting six months to one year can save a significant amount of money. Remember to look closely at all of the rates: the initial teaser rate, the true rate and the maximum rate. Review the periodic and lifetime caps as well. Things can change quickly for singles, due to issues such as job changes, career transition and marriage. During this transition period, an adjustable rate mortgage could make sense. Getting a 3/1 or 5/1 adjustable rate mortgage can lock you in at a lower rate and give you some peace of mind about the future as well. Ask your lender if the mortgage is assumable. Although assumable mortgages (in which a mortgage is transferred with no change in terms, and the buyer assumes all responsibility for repayment) are scarce these days, it doesn't hurt to ask.

If this is your first home, don't forget about Fannie Mae and Freddie Mac programs that offer low down payments and lower interest rate payments to first-time home buyers. There are certain income ceilings in place to qualify, but if you are beneath them, this is a great way to lock in a low-cost, low-interest loan. If you do put less than 20 percent down, you'll need to buy private mortgage insurance, or PMI. The amount you pay for PMI is based on a variety of factors such as the loan amount, loan type and the percentage of the down payment. If you'd like to see some specific numbers, plug your personal information into one of the many PMI calculators available online.

Considerations for Newlyweds

This is another population that tends to move quickly, particularly when the children start arriving. For those who want to buy a new home and start a family, investment advisors recommend focusing on wealth creation, not debt reduction at the expense of net worth. One of the most reliable ways to build net worth is to buy a home.

Before you make this important transaction, have a serious talk with your spouse about what each other's expectations are after the children arrive. Does one of you plan on staying home or working only part-time? When determining how much you can afford, estimate the income stream at each stage of your lives together, and remember to factor in closing, moving, and other costs.

Keep in mind that while you're young, time is on your side regarding investments. It's wise to contribute as much as you can to your 401(k) retirement plan so that the money can compound over time and build for retirement. Mortgage lenders say that no one ever asks for less than the amount for which they are approved. If you have other goals, be the exception. The maximum mortgage may not be the right one for you. Keep your other long-range goals in mind.

Fannie Mae and Freddie Mac programs might be an option if one of you has never bought a home before.

Considerations for Families

Unlike singles and newlyweds, families tend to stay in a home for a long time. Fixed rate loans are ideal for the long-term borrower. If they are within a percentage point of adjustable rates, the peace of mind involved in a fixed rate may be worth it. On the other hand, those who keep an adjustable rate mortgage for as long as 20 years often see their rates go higher and lower than a fixed rate. The great advantage of the adjustable rate loan over the long term is that the payment amount fluctuates every adjustment period to reflect the amount of principal paid on the loan.

With a fixed rate loan, you'll make the same payment at the beginning of the loan that you'll make at the very end of it. If you have the cash to endure the higher interest rates that an adjustable will invariably cycle through, in the long run, you may end up paying less than if you had chosen a fixed interest loan.

Considerations for Retirees

It may be appealing to head into retirement debt-free and without a mortgage payment. But saying goodbye to your mortgage also means saying goodbye to your best tax write-off! Even if you're not working, you can write off your mortgage interest expense against your dividend interest income. If your savings or other assets could easily pay off your mortgage, it's not necessary to take that step. Your other investments and savings are most likely getting a higher return than what it costs to pay the mortgage. For most homeowners, it almost makes sense to keep a mortgage. If, on the other hand, you don't have enough income to pay your monthly payments, you could consider a reverse mortgage, where the bank loans you equity in the form of monthly payments for a fixed period of time, usually 10 to 20 years.

PREAPPROVAL PREPARATION

If you've talked to an agent already, chances are you've been prequalified. In other words, the agent asked you a few questions about your income and assets and then gave you an estimate of how much of a mortgage you could afford. Prequalification gives you an idea of what you'll be able to afford and what your credit score is (most lenders will pull your credit report), and you'll start understanding which loan may work the best for your situation.

Preapproval is a more in-depth process. In this scenario, the lender has gone over your income documents and made sure that what you've stated is correct. It's important to get preapproval, particularly in a hot housing market. It shows the seller that you are a serious buyer and that there will be no trouble when it comes to closing the loan. You are better able to bargain for the house because you are a strong candidate. Another advantage of preapproval is that closing time will go more quickly and smoothly. When you get preapproved, much of your paperwork gets done.

SIGNS OF A GOOD LENDER

There are thousands of lenders out there, from mom-and-pop shops to global corporations. With all that competition, lenders should be offering the best "products" (loans) they can. You don't have to go with the first lender who comes your way. Here are some signs of lenders who are reputable and competitive:

They offer local approval. Good lenders don't send your loan application to a loan committee in the next state. When the lender knows the neighborhood and the market in the area, it can pull some strings with appraisal values, loan amounts and other mortgage issues on the dividing line. It's also beneficial to have a lending agent who is working face to face with your real estate agent. You are more likely to get favorable treatment with local talent than when you're no more than a loan number on a document. The agent, who may have a good track record with the lender, can discuss certain situations (such as bad credit or a low appraisal) with the lending agent on a personal level. More importantly, a distant lender can have all kinds of requirements that aren't typical in your state. In fact, there may not even be a form for what they request. Your confusion and scampering to figure out what is requested could cause you to lose the loan.

They are unafraid of competition. If a loan agent starts talking down to you, tries to throw out a bunch of confusing terms or doesn't explain what you've asked them to go over, then find another lender. A good loan agent will help you compare their loans to quotes from their competitors. Don't be shy to ask him/her to match the lowest interest rate you can find. They can always say no. But they may say yes, in which case you get a good lender and a low rate.

They are reliable. A good lender meets contract deadlines and even keeps you apprised of what you need to get, as well as where and when you need to get it. If you miss your deadlines, you could lose the house.

They guarantee no prepayment penalties. If the lender penalizes you for prepaying, you can find plenty of lenders who won't. Prepaying your mortgage (paying more than you initially agreed to pay on each payment) is a good way to shorten your mortgage term and save money. The lender generally would like you to borrow from them for as long as possible so that they can continue receiving your fees (your mortgage payment) for borrowing their money. Therefore, they'd most likely prefer it if you kept the loan as long as possible.

QUESTIONS TO ASK LENDERS

Lenders are used to borrowers pushing for reduced rates or lower points, fees, etc. There is probably not a question you could ask that they haven't heard before. You might want to consider asking:

- What types of loans do you offer?

- How many points do you charge for that rate?

- How much does the interest rate decrease if I pay one point? Two points?

- Do the locked-in rates apply at application or at approval?

- Does the lock-in include both the interest rate and the points and fees?

- Is there a charge for locking in the rate?

- If rates drop and I'm locked in at a higher rate, can I close at the lower rate? (Hold firm on this one—threaten to walk out. Most lenders will negotiate.)

- What is the processing time for the loan? (The average is 21 to 60 days.)

- Can you make a list of all your fees and email it to me? (Including application, credit report, appraisal, loan origination, etc.)

- Does the loan require personal mortgage insurance? How much is it? Can it be financed?

- Can the points and fees be financed?

- What are the escrow requirements?

- Are any special inspections required for this type of loan?

- What documents do I need to qualify for this loan?

WHAT TO DO IF YOUR LOAN GETS DENIED

When your loan gets denied, it helps to step back and think of some ways to get around your financial shortcomings. There are a number of ways you can do this. Among them:

Build up your down payment. With a higher down payment, say 25 percent to 30 percent, some mortgage lenders will get you through on their "no-income-verification" loan. While these usually have higher interest rates, you can consider refinancing at some point down the road when your income increases. This should be called the "rich relative" option, because if your income isn't high enough to qualify for your loan amount, chances are the only way you're going to get a big down payment is through the kindness of relatives.

Get a cosigner. Getting a cosigner on your loan is another way of turning the rejecting bank around. The lender will have somewhere to go (recourse) if you default on your loan. If you do make late payments or default, you'll damage both your and your cosigner's credit history. Because of this risk, do everything in your power to protect your cosigner. Insist on writing up a loan agreement and making the terms favorable to the cosigner.

Shop around for another lender. With the thousands of lenders out there, you might just have to work a little harder for one who will understand your situation and decide to take a chance on you. Mortgage brokers may know just which lenders can help someone with your income and circumstances. Remember, it's usually the savings and loans and smaller loan companies that offer the better rates.

Provide evidence to the lender of your imminent income increase. If you know you can afford that house because your stock options are coming due in three months or because you are in for a big bonus, just let the lender know. Provide reliable documentation and even some phone numbers for verification. Evidence of your upcoming windfall only increases your chances of getting the loan. If you have fixed cost of living increases (like many teachers and government employees), show documentation of that. A boss who has promised a salary increase needs to put it in writing so that you can show it to the mortgage company. Let them have just enough evidence to get your loan approved by the powers that be.

Look for alternative financing. When you are $10,000 to $30,000 short, it may be in your best interest to consider asking the seller to finance the loan. In which case, you should know about the seller "carryback." Sometimes, to get out of a house and on with their lives, a seller will act as a bank, loaning you an amount of money in exchange for interest payments and the promise of a payoff in a certain number of years (typically five to ten years).

Why would a seller want to carry a loan when a house sale is supposed to be a windfall of cash? Because the seller can make a respectable return on his or her investment. If the buyer defaults on the loan, the home reverts to the seller rather than to a lender. In fact, even if the lender gives you $200,000, the first owner is always considered to be the "first" on the loan. The seller has the most power.

Let's say you do default. The seller has enjoyed many months of interest payments and now gets to re-list the house under entirely new circumstances. The house gets to be a "new listing" once again. There are some decent perks to holding a small (not a large) seller "carryback" loan. Of course, this kind of loan requires an ironclad agreement drafted by a real estate lawyer. In a cool or slow housing market, you may want to propose this idea to the seller, particularly if you don't have the last $10,000. Seller "carrybacks" are often in the amount of $10,000 to $30,000. It wouldn't hurt to ask.

Another option is to look into other loan products. You could qualify for an adjustable rate mortgage or a piggyback loan. If that makes you too anxious, remember that you can refinance to a fixed rate a few years later.

ADDRESSING DEBT CONCERNS

While your income may be impressive, your overall debt ratio could disqualify you from getting the amount of money you would need to move into your dream home. If you can't pay down the debt enough to get your mortgage right now, you can buy a less expensive home, put yourself on a strict budget or get financial help. Sometimes mortgage lenders make debt payment a condition of the loan.

If you're feeling the pinch, it might help to take a quick inventory of the financial issues that you need to get under control before you take on the added responsibility of a home loan. Use the following brief worksheet to get it all down on paper.

Use the space below to record any issues that must be resolved for loan approval, and then set a goal for when you would like to have each problem taken care of:

Issues To Be Resolved   Date To Be Resolved

1. _____

2. _____

3. _____

4. _____

5. _____

6. _____

7. _____

8. _____

9. _____

10. _____

ADDRESSING APPRAISAL PREDICAMENTS

The appraiser comes in to reassure the bank that the home is worth what you are willing to pay for it. The lender orders the appraisal for good reason. The prospect of clients defaulting on loans is always on their minds. Sometimes, even when your finances are in tip-top shape, the house itself can be a problem. Lenders will only loan you a certain percentage of the value of the house. Most commonly, this number is 95 percent. Lenders want to make sure the loan is in sync with the property appraisal. If, in a tight market, you offered far more than what the comparable houses show it's worth, the bank may turn down the loan.

The appraisal could come in lower because the house needs some type of repair. You can ask the owner to make this repair and then present it in writing to the lender. Indication of the owner's intent to repair could sway the lender. An attorney should review this document.

Most Importantly …

The main point to keep in mind from this chapter is that you can question a lender or mortgage broker about every specific term you need. If you are uncertain about your future, the adjustable loan could be the way to go. If you're unsure about the economy's future direction, you may want to lock in a fixed rate.

NOTES

FIXED RATE MORTGAGES

The fixed rate loan offers a special premium: Peace of mind. Your payment today will be the same payment you'll make each month for the next thirty years. You pay a higher interest rate than you do with an adjustable loan because, in this scenario, it's the lender that takes on the greater risk. If interest rates climb, the lender is stuck earning only the rate agreed upon for 20 to 30 years. If interest rates drop, you can always refinance. You're NOT stuck at all. The lender agrees to keep the rate at a certain point, even if interest rates rise. This is the opposite of an adjustable rate mortgage, where the bank is free to raise your rate (although, as mentioned, you can always refinance to a fixed rate loan).

THE PROS AND CONS OF A FIXED RATE MORTGAGE

When interest rates are low and close to adjustable rate levels, it makes sense to get a fixed rate loan. But how low is low? The only way to gauge rates is to look at them historically. In the 1980s, rates often went as high as 14 percent. By 1990, fixed mortgage rates hovered around 10 percent. They continued to drop until the years from 2002 to 2004, when fixed rate loans could be found at 6 percent and adjustables in the 4 percent range. The phrase "the lowest rates in 40 years" blared all over the news. Rates between 6 percent and 7 percent are considered low.

To gauge whether a mortgage rate is indeed low (or a good buy, so to speak) look at the rate of return on other investments over the past century. Stocks have returned 10 percent per year (in the past 15 years, they've returned 11.5 percent). Less risky investments like treasury bills, bonds and certificates of deposit usually reward buyers with returns from 4 percent to 7 percent. When mortgage rates climb higher than the rate of return on stocks, you know that they're high and perhaps ready to begin their descent. That's when an adjustable mortgage would make more sense.

The disadvantage of this type of loan is that if you acquire a fixed rate mortgage and rates start going way down, you may regret your move. The stability of a fixed rate loan comes at the price of possibly missing some money-saving opportunities when interest rates fluctuate in the homeowner's favor.

FIXED RATE MORTGAGES

BALANCING INTEREST RATES AND UP-FRONT FEES

Lenders make their money on loans from up-front points and fees and, over the long term, with interest payments. You get the advantage of lower interest rates when you pay substantial fees up front in a move called "buying down" the rate. Lenders call these fees "points." If you don't have any more cash for points and fees, you will not be able to secure the lower interest rate. But you won't be out the initial several thousand dollars either.

When considering a fixed rate loan, borrowers weigh up-front fees or "points" against the interest rate. Points can run from 0 to 2 percent of the loan amount. A $500,000 loan at 1 point would cost you $5,000. A $500,000 loan at 2 points would cost you $10,000. On top of that, you pay additional closing costs, the amount of which varies from state to state.

Points and interest rates are inversely proportional. In other words, you pay more points for a lower rate. If you can pay more points up front, you have a lower rate. If your cash is stretched to the max, you may have to settle with a higher interest rate since you are not in the position to "buy down" the loan.

WARNING! Don't let "no-cost" loans dazzle you. They are not always a good deal. If you pay less in points, the ongoing interest rate will be higher. In general, lenders who push no-point loans aren't the most competitive lenders in the business. Consider no-point loans only when you are budgeting every penny for the home down payment and if you don't plan on keeping the mortgage for the long term.

GETTING THE BEST TERM ON A FIXED RATE LOAN

When deciding how long to keep your loan, take into consideration factors such as your own financial situation, personality and investment sophistication. The biggest bonus for a 30-year mortgage as opposed to a 15-year mortgage is that it requires lower monthly payments. You can use your money to invest in the stock market or pursue other financial goals.

The most successful investors "diversify." In other words, they invest in several areas: real estate, stocks, bonds and certificates of deposit. Often, when one investment does poorly, the other sectors do well. This happens because people are "looking for a place to put their money." If stocks look weak, people may "flee" into treasury bills because they have a guaranteed return of at least a few percentage points. When CDs offer only 4 percent interest, investors think they surely can get a better return in the stock market. Then stocks start rising. As with real estate, the return on investments depends on supply and demand.

Even if you can afford a 15-year mortgage, you may not want to sink all of your money into your house, especially if you don't have much saved for retirement. Money that you put into your 401(k) and 403(b) plans at work (and the SEP IRAs or Keoghs for the self-employed) give you an immediate reduction in taxes and enable your interest to compound, tax-deferred.

Basically, if you want to view your home as a real estate investment and load it up with capital, get that 15-year loan. More of your money goes into your home. If other investments or a home-based business call, go with the 30-year loan. The biggest advantage in choosing a 15-year term for your mortgage is that the interest rate may be slightly lower. The shorter the mortgage term, the less risk the bank takes.

When making your decision, keep in mind that since 1980, the stock market has returned 11.5 percent per year while home prices have appreciated by 9 percent. That's a pretty close race. Homes also give owners the immediate benefit of food and shelter. To play it safe, investors should have money in retirement accounts, real estate and other investment instruments.

The other benefit of the 30-year loan is that it can act like a 20- or 15-year loan. It all depends on how much extra you are willing to put into your mortgage payment each month. With a 30-year loan, you usually have the option of "prepaying" or "paying down" your mortgage. This means that you can pay more than you initially signed on to pay. This extra payment goes straight to your principal to diminish it. Before you "pay down" the loan, make sure you don't have any "prepayment penalties" where the lender actually charges you for paying off some of the principal. If you do, you may need to negotiate these fees down. Chronic savers love the 15-year program. Monthly payments run 20 percent to 30 percent higher than the 30-year option. Believe it or not, lenders offer mortgages with terms of 7, 10 and 20 years. You can lock yourself into one of these to make yourself save.

WARNING! Sometimes lenders or agents may scare you away from the 30-year mortgage by citing figures that show (due to compounding interest over the 30-year term) that you basically pay three times what you initially borrowed. That is true. However, because you did not have to pay for your home up front, you might have been able to use the bank's money to make more money for yourself by building up your investment portfolio. If you have some money to invest early on, you can let time compound it for you. In the end, time compounds cash faster than the mortgage can eat it up.

FIXED RATE MORTGAGES

WORKING YOUR MONEY

Some investors are mortgaged to the hilt, and they sleep just fine at night. They don't mind paying the bank 7 percent so that they can use its money to invest in something else for a 10 percent return. For instance, some borrowers will borrow an additional $100,000 from the bank to put on their mortgage, even if they have $100,000 in their savings account. They invest that $100,000 into a stock. By the end of the year, they have paid the bank 7 percent or $7,000 for the privilege of using their money. When they sell their stock, they sell it for $110,000, a $10,000 profit. They are ahead of the game by $3,000.

However, $3,000 may not be worth the risk for you. What if the investor turned out to be wrong and the stock only rose 5 percent. The investor would have paid out 7 percent or $7,000 and earned only 5 percent or $5,000. The investor would have lost $2,000 that year. You don't want to even consider the penalties if the stock lost 20 percent of its value that year and the investor had to sell it and pay the bank the $7,000 fee for using their money. Some investors make their living working these kinds of point spreads.

PAYING MONTHLY OR BIWEEKLY MORTGAGES

Lenders will often give you the option of paying by the month or every two weeks on 30-year loans. Since there are 52 weeks in the year, you make two extra payments a year when paying biweekly. These extra payments reduce your loan term to 24 years, a happy medium between a 15-year mortgage and a 30-year mortgage. Of course, you can accomplish the same thing by making two extra payments every year on your regular 30-year mortgage without being tied into the biweekly program.

MORTGAGE PAYMENT CALCULATOR

The following table will help you determine your mortgage payment based on the loan amount. Follow the simple steps to calculate your monthly payments.

Step 1: Take the amount of money you would like to borrow and divide it by 1,000.

Step 2: Follow the row corresponding to the interest rate your lender is currently offering to the 15-year mortgage or the 30-year mortgage column, depending on which you plan to apply for, and find the appropriate number.

Step 3: Multiply the number you got in Step 1 by the number you got in Step 2. The resulting figure will be your mortgage payment. For example, if you want a loan amount of $400,000, start by dividing that by 1,000. This will give you 400. Now, let's say that your bank is offering you a 30-year loan at a 6.5% fixed rate. The multiplication factor under the 30-year mortgage column for the 6.5% interest rate is 6.33. Now multiply 400 by 6.33 and you will get that your monthly mortgage payment will be $2,532. This would be your Principal + Interest, or PI.

Interest Rate	15-year Mortgage	30-year Mortgage
4	7.40	4.77
4 ½	7.65	5.07
5	7.91	5.37
5 ½	8.18	5.68
6	8.44	6.00
6 ½	8.72	6.33
7	8.99	6.65
7 ½	9.28	7.00
8	9.56	7.34
8 ½	9.85	7.69
9	10.15	8.05
9 ½	10.45	8.41
10	10.75	8.78
10 ½	11.06	9.15
11	11.37	9.53
11 ½	11.69	9.91
12	12.01	10.29
12 ½	12.17	10.4

FIXED RATE MORTGAGE

FIXED RATE MORTGAGE

As we have discussed, the monthly payments on a fixed rate mortgage are always the same. What changes is the amount of principal and interest paid in each payment. During the early years in the life of your loan, most of your monthly payment goes toward paying interest and very little goes toward paying off the actual loan. But as you make payments over the years, more money goes toward paying off your loan; since the amount owed becomes less, the interest charged is less. To illustrate this, we have laid out a table showing the amount of principal and interest that are paid in the first 12 months and in the last 12 months for the following loan:

- Amount of the loan: $100,000
- Duration of the loan: 30 years
- Payments per year: 12
- Annual interest rate: 7%

According to the mortgage calculator on the following page, your monthly payment would be $665. More precisely, it would be $665.30. If you look at the next table, you can see the amount of money that is actually applied toward principal and interest in your $665.30 payment for the first and last 12 months. It is interesting to note that in your first payment, only $81.97 is going toward the principal and $583.33 is going toward the interest. In your last payment, $661.31 is going toward the principal and only $3.86 is going toward the interest.

To calculate this, you need to multiply the amount of money owed on any given month by your interest rate. In this case, when you make your first payment, you owe $100,000 at the 7 percent interest rate; therefore, you would multiply $100,000 x .07 and divide this number by 12 months. This will give you $583.33, or the amount of money that you pay in interest during the first month of that loan. To find the amount of money that goes toward the principal of your loan, you need to subtract the amount of money that went toward the interest from your monthly payment. $665.30 - $583.33 = $81.97.

Now, for the next month, the actual amount owed is $100,000 minus $81.97 or $99,918.03. Since you owe less money in the second month, less of your payment will go toward the interest and more toward the principal. This continues each month until the end of the 30-year term. You start paying more money toward your principal and less money toward interest after 21.1 years or 253 payments.

It is also interesting to note the amount of money in interest that you will pay in 30 years. In this example, you end up paying $139,508.75 in interest for your $100,000 loan. That's why we recommend that you pay your loan as fast as you can by making a few extra payments each year. A fixed rate mortgage is usually considered a long-term loan and works best for home buyers who plan on keeping their property for 15 years or more.

Payment schedule for a $100,000 loan at 7% interest, 30-year fix mortgage:

Monthly Payment #	Interest Rate	Payment Amount	Interest Portion	Principal Reduction	Mortgage Balance
1	7%	$665.30	$583.33	$81.97	$99,918.03
2	7%	$665.30	$582.86	$82.45	$99,835.59
3	7%	$665.30	$582.37	$82.93	$99,752.66
4	7%	$665.30	$581.89	$83.41	$99,669.24
5	7%	$665.30	$581.40	$83.90	$99,585.34
6	7%	$665.30	$580.91	$84.39	$99,500.95
7	7%	$665.30	$580.42	$84.88	$99,416.07
8	7%	$665.30	$579.93	$85.38	$99,330.70
9	7%	$665.30	$579.43	$85.87	$99,244.82
10	7%	$665.30	$578.93	$86.37	$99,158.45
11	7%	$665.30	$578.42	$86.88	$99,071.57
12	7%	$665.30	$577.92	$87.39	$98,984.19

Monthly Payment #	Interest Rate	Payment Amount	Interest Portion	Principal Reduction	Mortgage Balance
349	7%	$665.30	$44.85	$620.45	$7,068.40
350	7%	$665.30	$41.23	$624.07	$6,444.33
351	7%	$665.30	$37.59	$627.71	$5,816.62
352	7%	$665.30	$33.93	$631.37	$5,185.25
353	7%	$665.30	$30.25	$635.06	$4,550.19
354	7%	$665.30	$26.54	$638.76	$3,911.43
355	7%	$665.30	$22.82	$642.49	$3,268.95
356	7%	$665.30	$19.07	$646.23	$2,622.71
357	7%	$665.30	$15.30	$650.00	$1,972.71
358	7%	$665.30	$11.51	$653.79	$1,318.92
359	7%	$665.30	$7.69	$657.61	$661.31
360	7%	$665.17	$3.86	$661.31	0.00

FIXED RATE LENDER CONTACT INFORMATION WORKSHEET

Use this worksheet to record contact information for the lenders that you have interviewed and to make notes on what their references have said about them. This will allow you to choose a lender that is right for you.

	Lender #1	Lender #2	Lender #3	Lender #4
Name of Company				
Contact's Name				
Company Address				
Phone Number				
Email Address				
Web Address				
Reference #1 Name Phone number				
Reference #2 Name Phone number				
Reference #3 Name Phone number				
Reference #4 Name Phone number				

FIXED RATE MORTGAGE COMPARISON WORKSHEET

Use this worksheet to compare the interest rate and fees that various lenders can offer you for a fixed rate mortgage.

	Lender #1	Lender #2	Lender #3	Lender #4
Company Name				
Contact Person				
Phone #				
Email				
Lender Interest				
Points				
Monthly Payment				
15 Years Fixed Rate				
30 Years Fixed Rate				
Minimum Down Payment				
Loan Amount				
Loan Origination Fee				
Prepayment Penalty				
Application Fee				
FICO Score Required				
Additional Comments				

NOTES

ADJUSTABLE RATE MORTGAGES

Americans have typically been cautious about the adjustable rate mortgage (or ARM), whereas the British, Australians and New Zealanders choose them without a moment's hesitation. In fact, in those countries, adjustables are far more common than fixed rate loans. Even if you've always been leery about adjustables, take the time to go over this section. It's good to know as much as you can about as many types of loans as you can. You may find a way to save hundreds of dollars every month with little—or at least acceptable—risk. Use the *My Mortgage Terms and Limits Worksheet* on page 92 to find out which mortgage is right for you.

ADVANTAGES OF AN ADJUSTABLE RATE MORTGAGE

Most adjustable rate mortgages have a short-term fixed rate period when the interest rate is always lower—and sometimes significantly lower—than a fixed rate mortgage.

One-year ARMs used to be the most popular adjustable. Now there are three-year, five-year, seven-year and ten-year ARMs (also called "hybrid" loans) that work well for many home buyers. After the initial or "teaser" period ends (usually in six months to two years), the rate jumps to its "true" rate. One-year ARMs have their first adjustment after one year. For the three-year adjustable, the fixed rate stays the same for three years and then adjusts annually after that. The five, seven and ten year adjustables stay fixed for five, seven or ten years respectively and then adjust annually every year thereafter. The longer the fixed period of the loan, the less risk you take. Less risk, however, translates into higher interest rates and fees.

DISADVANTAGES OF AN ADJUSTABLE RATE MORTGAGE

The challenge with the adjustable loan is the inherent guessing game that both you and the bank or lender engage in while watching interest rates. Everyone is guessing whether interest rates will go up or down. ARMs benefit home buyers if interest rates start going down after the loan is assumed. When interest rates go up, the lender (which is already benefiting greatly from your business) gains even more.

ADJUSTABLE RATE MORTGAGES

ADJUSTING FOR PEAKS AND VALLEYS

Mortgage lenders give you a break with an adjustable mortgage because you do take the risk that the interest rates may rise. If they go up, so does your mortgage payment. It's not pocket change, either. An extra two or even three hundred dollars each month can be enough to make it impossible to pay your mortgage payment, and you could go into default.

Remember, there's a reason why that initial period is called the "teaser" rate. It gets your attention and stimulates you to respond to it—but it also has the potential to get you in trouble.

STAYING ON TOP OF INTEREST RATES

Mortgage lenders set their loan interest rates according to institutional monetary instruments known as indexes. These financial calculations follow the Federal Reserve's manipulation of the federal funds rate.

The Federal Reserve often raises rates when the economy is doing very well and inflation threatens to send prices of goods and services skyrocketing. The Federal Reserve lowers rates when the economy isn't doing so well—when workers are being laid off and factories are closing. The lower interest rate is an incentive to get both businesses and people borrowing money to spend again and fuel the economy.

From early 2001 to mid-2003 (after the stock market bubble burst and layoffs were rampant), the Federal Reserve lowered its interest rate thirteen times to fight recession. During that time, mortgage rates dropped, with some fixed rates going as low as 5 percent, which was the lowest level since 1958. The lower mortgage rates helped fuel the dramatic rise in house prices during the early part of the new millennium. Home equity swelled. Feeling "house rich," owners took out home equity loans, and the economy recovered.

Most likely, your interest rate will rise and fall with the federal funds rate. Like the federal funds rate, the index rises and falls, reflecting the interest rates of certain financial instruments. The most common index underlying adjustable rate mortgages is the "cost of funds" index. A cost of funds index (COFI) is a regional average of interest expenses incurred by financial institutions, which are used as a basis for calculating variable rate loans. This index is set by a self-regulatory agency such as the Federal Home Loan Banks. Interest rates on COFI loans and mortgages can fluctuate more slowly than those on loans linked to other indexes.

You can find the current cost of funds by looking in your local newspaper. If you do choose an adjustable rate mortgage, you can keep your lender honest by following that number yourself. If the cost of funds index declines and your adjustable mortgage rate does not, you are well within your rights to give your lender a call.

If your lender doesn't tie your loan to the cost of funds index, it may use another index like the rate of sales on treasury notes and bills, the average rate for loans closed or the average rate paid on jumbo CDs.

YOUR ADJUSTABLE RATE MORTGAGE'S "TRUE" RATE

Despite being tickled about your low initial or teaser interest rate, you need to take a hard look at what will be the "true" interest rate. The true interest rate is derived by adding the index the loan is based on to the lender's "margin." The lender adds a margin, an additional percentage, in order to cover its expenses and to make a profit. It is not out-of-line to come right out and ask your lender what their margin is. A margin can be anywhere from 1 to 5 percent. If the cost of funds (assuming that's what your loan is tied to) for the day is 3.9 percent and the lender's margin is 1.7 percent, then the interest rate on your adjustable will be 5.6 percent.

If the mortgage lender or broker keeps bringing up the initial rate, try to get them to focus on the true rate: the index on which the loan is based, plus the margin. Even ask what the payment on the amount of loan you are looking at would be like for that very day one year in the future. Ask them the payment at the initial rate, the true rate and at the maximum rate.

HOW RISKY IS YOUR MORTGAGE RATE?

In reality, ARMs are not as dangerous as one might think. When people think "interest rates," the other term that most often comes up is "skyrocketing." Because of both the "periodic cap" and the "lifetime cap" on ARMs, interest rates can't soar into the stratosphere at warp speed. After the first initial teaser rate period expires, the interest rate is allowed to adjust according to its periodic cap, which is typically at 2 percent. Therefore, your interest rate cannot climb higher than 2 percent each year.

This may sound like a lot! It would be, if not for the lifetime cap, which limits how high the interest rate can go over the life of the mortgage. Most ARMs have a lifetime cap of 5 percent to 6 percent. For example, consider a mortgage with an initial rate of 4.5 percent, a periodic cap of 2 percent and a lifetime cap of 5 percent. The interest rate on this loan for the first year is 4.5 percent; the second year, it could go as high as 6.5 percent (depending on the movement of its index). In the third year for this same loan, the interest rate could go as high as 8.5 percent. In the fourth year and every year thereafter, your loan cannot go any higher than 9.5 percent.

ADJUSTABLE RATE MORTGAGES

The adjustable rate mortgage can get you into a bigger house and help you buy a short-term investment property. Always follow the federal funds rate and the index to which your loan is tied. You should also have a firm grasp on the different kinds of rates involved in your loan: the initial rate and the periodic and lifetime caps. With this simple knowledge, you can work an adjustable rate mortgage to your advantage.

IS AN ADJUSTABLE LOAN RIGHT FOR YOU?

Adjustable rate mortgages intimidate some and excite others. If you can assess the risk and understand the economy, you'll be more comfortable with an adjustable rate mortgage or ARM than a home buyer who is skittish and invests only in things like CDs with guaranteed returns.

Many people find that the only way to get in on a certain house is to go for the adjustable. If this is the case for you, make sure you ask your lender what your highest possible monthly payment could be during any time over the period of the loan. Listen closely to make sure you can afford the increased mortgage payment in three to five years. A little advance knowledge could make the difference between keeping or losing the house. It's best to know what you're getting into now and in the future.

The following types of people might consider an adjustable rate mortgage.

Someone expecting an increase in income: Banks and brokers like to offer adjustable rate mortgages to young professionals at the beginning of their careers. While the mortgage payment seems like a stretch to this group, their incomes generally rise over the years. Once they're earning more, the percentage of their gross monthly income going to housing becomes more manageable.

Risk takers: If taking risks has worked out well for you in the past, you may feel the pull of an adjustable mortgage. While adjustable mortgages may seem risky, interest rates do go up and down. Make sure you can afford to ride the highs and the lows. If you stick to the ARM throughout the life of the loan, you'll most likely pay less over the long run. Remember, just because you signed the mortgage documents for an adjustable loan doesn't mean you are tied to it for the rest of your life. You can always refinance into a fixed rate loan, as many people do.

Granted, there will be points, fees and closing costs, but these you can always feed into the loan amount. You will probably pay some fees, but if interest rates are going up quickly, it may be worth it to refinance into a more stable mortgage. While refinancing is not the outcome you necessarily want (you were hoping rates would go down), it does cut the perceived risk of an ARM. But keep in mind that when you are ready to finance, the fixed rate available at that time may be much higher than when you got your adjustable rate.

Real estate investors: The majority of those who invest in real estate go with an adjustable rate mortgage. This is particularly true for investors wanting to find fixer-uppers to refurbish and sell. They probably won't keep the property longer than two to three years. It makes the most sense to take advantage of the low teaser rate, which usually lasts a year. With the second and third years limited by the periodic cap.

Short-term owners: Saving money in the first two to three years is almost guaranteed with an adjustable rate mortgage. These kinds of loans have not only lower initial interest rates, but also lower closing costs. If you're buying a home just to get into the market and build a bigger down payment for your dream home, an adjustable would make sense. You get into trouble, however, when time goes by and the adjustable gets murky. But that's the risk you take with this kind of loan. While interest rates don't move too fast over a five- to seven-year period, you will still be looking at substantially higher payments than you had when you started.

Remember, most adjustable mortgages have a cap of no more than a 2 percent increase per year, with it going no higher than 6 percent above the original rate over the life of the loan. If you are uncertain about your time period in a home, the hybrid loans, which are adjustable for several years and then convert to a fixed rate, may work for you.

Thrifty homeowners: Because adjustable loans can increase dramatically, they work well mostly for those who are borrowing less than the bank says they can borrow. People who are consistently saving 10 percent of their income have the cash cushion needed should interest rates go up. Thrifty homeowners will also appreciate the fact that, if they pay extra toward the principal, the adjustable loan registers a reduction in principal when it readjusts every year, thereby reducing the monthly payments. The payments of an owner with a fixed rate loan are based on the interest on the amount initially borrowed. To lower the monthly payment, the fixed rate loan owner would have to pay points, fees and closing costs, unlike the borrower with an ARM.

GETTING THE BEST DEAL ON EACH COMPONENT OF THE ARM

You can negotiate the components of an ARM. You have even more leverage if you are familiar with everything that they imply. For example, mortgage brokers and lenders often portray their rates as set in stone. Despite their firm statements ("This is what Bank of America is offering today"), you can get them to come down a bit if you are a good candidate. It might also be helpful to know that the biggest, most advertised banks usually don't have the best rates. Smaller banks and mortgage bankers that stick strictly to mortgages, savings and loans tend to do better.

ADJUSTABLE RATE MORTGAGES

QUESTIONS TO ASK YOUR LENDER ABOUT AN ARM

- What is the initial teaser rate?

- What is the true rate (index + margin)?

- What is the periodic cap?

- What is the lifetime cap?

- What is the index based on?

- How long does the initial rate last?

- What is the maximum amount I can pay per month?

- Can I convert the loan to a fixed rate loan? When can I do that? Would there be a fee to convert to a fixed loan?

ARM LENDER CONTACT INFORMATION WORKSHEET

Use this worksheet to record contact information for the lenders that you have interviewed and to make notes on what their references have said about them.

	Company #1	Company #2	Company #3	Company #4
Name of Company				
Contact's Name				
Company Address				
Phone Number				
Email Address				
Web Address				
Reference #1 Name Phone number				
Reference #2 Name Phone number				
Reference #3 Name Phone number				
Reference #4 Name Phone number				

ADJUSTABLE RATE MORTGAGE PAYMENT WORKSHEET

Use the following two worksheets to compare the interest rates and fees that various lenders can offer you for an adjustable rate mortgage. Then use the Mortgage Payment Calculator on page 79 to determine if you can afford the worst case scenario for the first five years of your loan.

	Lender #1	Lender #2
Name of Company		
Loan Amount		
Initial Interest Rate		
True Interest Rate		
Periodic Cap		
Lifetime Cap		
Term		

First Five Years Worst Case Scenario

Year #1 Interest Rate = Monthly Payment =		
Year #2 Interest Rate + Periodic Cap= Monthly Payment =		
Year #3 Interest Rate + Periodic Cap= Monthly Payment =		
Year #4 Interest Rate + Periodic Cap= (Not to exceed starting rate plus lifetime cap) Monthly Payment =		
Year #5 Interest Rate + Periodic Cap= (Not to exceed starting rate plus lifetime cap) Monthly Payment =		

Lender #3	Lender #4	Lender #5

First Five Years Worst Case Scenario

MY MORTGAGE TERMS AND LIMITS WORKSHEET

Based on your research on loan rates, fees and terms, fill in just what you will pay for the following types of loans. These charts will help you choose the loan that is right for you.

Amount to Borrow: $

Adjustable Loan	Interest Rate	Points	Fees	Payment	Assumable? Y/N	Prepayment Penalties? Y/N
1-year						
3/1						
5/1						
7/1						

Two-Step	Interest Rate	Points	Fees	Payment	Assumable? Y/N	Prepayment Penalties? Y/N
7/23						
5/25						

Fixed Loan	Interest Rate	Points	Fees	Payment	Assumable? Y/N	Prepayment Penalties? Y/N
15-year						
30-year						

Top Three Loan Choices

Institution: Terms (rate, points, fees, payment):

_____   _____

_____   _____

_____   _____

_____   _____

_____   _____

OTHER HOME
FINANCING OPTIONS

Some home buyers prefer "creative financing." This is where seller financing, balloon mortgages, interest-only loans and two-step mortgages help out. These kinds of loans work well in the short term. The interest rate is usually lower than a fixed rate mortgage, and some are available with low or no points. If your income is insufficient to afford the house at a higher fixed rate or even through a hybrid loan, you may be stuck with this kind of loan.

In this chapter, we also cover VA loans and leasing with an option to buy. While these options are unrelated, it's important to know that they are available. It's a reminder that there are all kinds of ways to get into your dream home.

SELLER FINANCING

Every once in a while, you'll run across a real estate ad that indicates the seller will help you with financing. This is particularly true in a soft or declining housing market. In this arrangement, sellers can get higher interest rates from you than they can get from the bank. Older couples with a lot of equity in a house—cash they don't need right away—often trade getting a higher price for the risk of carrying a reasonable first or second mortgage for a short term. Sellers usually offer only five to ten year loan terms. Under this setup, you'll have to save up enough to both pay back the seller and build up enough equity to refinance the loan into a new 80 percent conventional mortgage. If you choose to go this route, do not settle for an interest rate higher than what you're paying to your traditional mortgage lender.

WARNING! Sellers eager enough to provide financing might simply be desperate to unload a problem home.

BALLOON MORTGAGE

Balloon mortgages begin at a big discount but pack a wallop at the end. The interest rate is generally lower, but the entire loan amount is due in full at the end of the initial period, which usually lasts three to ten years. Have you heard the expression "Borrowing from Peter to pay Paul?" Well that's essentially what you'll be doing under this scenario. You'll have to find another loan to pay off the balloon mortgage. You're in for a whole new round of closing costs, points and fees.

These kinds of mortgages do have their fans and may seem appealing in times of high interest rates when their rates are lower than fixed loans. If you don't plan on living in the home long, this could be an option. If you are planning on building up equity and reducing your loan term, you won't be very far along in those goals at the end of a balloon loan. Your plans can change, and if you're stuck with a balloon loan you could be in trouble.

Why? You could get trapped in a balloon loan if you are unable to get refinancing. This could happen if the property value drops significantly and your income declines. Combine this with rising interest rates that put your income-to-expense ratio below banks' standards, and you could be out of luck. In this case, you'd be forced to pay off the mortgage, and the only way to do so would be to sell the house. Refinancing is never guaranteed.

Only consider a balloon loan if you are certain that you will have the balance of the mortgage at the end of the initial fixed rate term.

INTEREST-ONLY LOANS

If you're a salesperson or an executive who gets huge bonuses a couple of times a year, you might consider this kind of mortgage. An interest-only mortgage loan means just that. You pay only the interest on the mortgage in monthly payments for a fixed term. After the end of that term, usually five to seven years, you either refinance, pay the balance in a lump sum or start paying off the principal, in which case the payments jump skyward.

A typical interest-only borrower is someone who earns a moderate salary and gets a huge bonus once or twice a year. The interest-only mortgage allows the borrower to pay down big chunks of principal when bonus time rolls around.

Here are some circumstances in which an interest-only mortgage might be a good fit:
• You have income mostly from infrequent commissions or bonuses
• You expect to earn a lot more in a few years
• You plan to invest the savings on the difference between an interest-only mortgage and an amortized mortgage
• You foresee values going up, and you want to get the most expensive house you can afford.

80-10-10 AND 80-15-5 MORTGAGES

This is another type of loan that works well if you know you will move within seven years. This kind of loan is actually made up of two loans. For example, the 80-10-10 loan requires a 10 percent down payment. One loan is in the amount of 80 percent of the total mortgage and is a fixed or adjustable mortgage. The second loan is in the amount of 10 percent of the mortgage, which is usually a balloon payment. The second 10 percent is paid in cash.

Why such a complicated loan arrangement? The bank sees this as a 20 percent down payment and waives the private mortgage insurance (PMI) payment. It can also move you from the higher interest rate of the jumbo loan category to a regular loan category with a lower interest rate. Jumbo loans are higher loan amounts than Fannie Mae and Freddie Mac will approve.

WARNING! Beware the "acceleration clause" in your mortgage loan contract. If you signed off on this stipulation, the lender has the right to demand payment of the entire outstanding mortgage balance if you miss a monthly payment, sell the property or breach a term in the contract. Make sure to ask your lender about whether there is an acceleration clause in your mortgage contract.

TWO-STEP MORTGAGES

The two-step loan is divided into two periods. Often the two-step is either a 5/25, with the initial period ending after five years, or a 7/23, with the initial period ending after seven years. During the first period, the interest rate is fixed and usually lower than a 30-year fixed mortgage rate. After the initial period expires, the rate is reset.

Most people refinance out of this type of loan before the initial period ends. Borrowers find products with more competitive rates than the rate offered for the second part of the loan.

These loans are the most useful when you're not sure how long you will stay in the home. When the initial period is over, the bank adjusts the rate to a fixed rate that's always higher than the initial rate. With interest payments lower than a 30-year fixed rate, you will be able to qualify for a higher mortgage amount. While this may sound appealing, you could get stuck with the higher adjusted rate mortgage if you cannot qualify for refinancing. The rate for the second period is usually around 1 percent higher than the fixed rate loans at the time of the adjustment.

When you apply for your loan, prepare for a flood of paperwork. One of the most important papers is the estimate of closing costs. When you go to close, you want to make sure all the fees are in the same range as originally quoted.

NEGATIVE AMORTIZATION LOANS

Negative amortization loans are not quite the payment option that many advertisers would like you to think they are; they're far from it. These loans calculate two interest rates. The first one is what's known as the "payment rate" and is typically capped at 7.5 percent. The second is the "true interest rate," which is calculated as simply the index, plus the margin without periodic caps.

Borrowers are given a choice of which interest rate to pay. Hence the advertisers' pitch of offering negative amortization loans as "payment option" loans. Sure, borrowers do have a payment option, which offers a degree of flexibility. But the borrower still has to pay the true interest rate. Also, when you don't make the full payment (the first payment rate), the rest of the payment is added to your loan balance. In other words, by exercising your option, you are increasing your loan balance. There's a reason we have a big warning below about negative amortization loans.

WARNING! Stay away from negative amortization. One term a lender may throw out is "Payment Cap." It almost sounds like a positive concept, but it's not. If your mortgage payment is initially $1,000 and interest rates skyrocket so that the payment climbs to $1,200 a month, you may be thrilled to hear that your payment cap is $1,150. Don't be. You are obligated to pay $1,200, but are only allowed to pay $1,150. The $50 is considered a debt you owe and is placed on the principal of the loan. Since each payment is part interest and part principal, you're in real trouble if interest rates rise at the beginning of the loan when the majority of each payment is interest. This situation is called "negative amortization" because your principal balance increases instead of decreases. When you are ready to sell your house, your loan may be a lot higher than the price at which you can sell your house.

When you find the loan that's right for you, be sure to ask your lender if there is any way you could get into a negative amortization scenario. If they hint that there could be, go to your next possible lender.

VETERANS AFFAIRS (VA) LOANS

Generally, VA loans are only available for veterans, active service members, reservists and members of public health service. As amazing as it sounds, these kinds of loans require no down payment and are available from most lenders. VA loans are limited to $240,000. Home buyers in high priced markets may need to look for other financing options. Also, if you apply for a VA loan, it's not a guarantee that you will get it. The loan is based on income, assets and debt history, as with any loan.

Another distinct advantage with a VA loan is that the government limits the amount of closing costs and origination fees lenders can charge, as well as the appraisal fees. Also, there is no private insurance. The interest rates follow the market like other home loans. VA loans do require a one-time funding fee that ranges from 1.25 percent to 3 percent, depending on the veteran's service and whether it's a first or subsequent loan.

LEASING WITH OPTION TO BUY

Often, leasing with an option to buy is considered with a second home/vacation property. But first-time buyers might also find it advantageous under the right circumstances. If you're not sure whether you should commit to buying a property that you already rent, this might be the way to go, providing the landlord wants to go this route as well.

These arrangements are typically set up where the potential buyer rents the property for a set period of time, typically a year, with the option to purchase it at a future date at a predetermined price. The monthly rent payment might be higher than regular rent. The "extra amount" that's tacked onto the rent is applied to the purchase price or is considered payment for the "right" or "option" to buy at the set price. Another way of viewing this extra amount is to think of it as equity.

LENDER CONTACT INFORMATION WORKSHEET

Record the following information for your top four lenders so that you can choose the lender that is right for you. You can also use this worksheet to write down what their references have to say.

	Company #1	Company #2	Company #3	Company #4
Name of Company				
Contact's Name				
Company Address				
Phone Number				
Email Address				
Interest				
Points				
Web Address				
Reference #1 Name Phone number				
Reference #2 Name Phone number				
Reference #3 Name Phone number				
Reference #4 Name Phone number				

PART 4:

FINDING YOUR DREAM HOME

WHAT MAKES A HOUSE A DREAM HOME

Let's get out of the world of dry facts and figures and get you started dreaming about your new neighborhood and home. Whether you're a single professional, a newlywed, a parent or a retiree, you can find the perfect home.

When most people decide they want to buy a house, they call a Realtor and go from house to house, determining which one strikes their fancy. In other words, they're waiting for an emotional reaction. Emotions are good, but it's best to get reason working in there, too. By taking some time to brainstorm just what your most important and least important needs and wants are, you're more likely to end up with a home that you will stay in for a long time. Those who stay put have the greatest chances of making the most money. They also avoid moving hassles and a couple of rounds of closing costs and property tax increases. These are major financial outlays. If you can do it right the first time, you will be much better off.

WHAT IS YOUR MOTIVATION?

Buying with Resale in Mind

Most advertisers know that, in order to make a sale, an ad or product needs to appeal to the emotions first. Then, it must make a reasonable argument in favor of the sale after that initial excitement wears off. When you're buying a home, you should use both emotion and reason. Your underlying motivation will tell you which aspect to depend on more heavily.

If you know this home won't be your last home, place more emphasis on practical arguments than emotions. Basically, you're buying this house in order to take advantage of the rising housing market. The house will suffice for the time being, but you want to build up a down payment to trade up to a larger home eventually. Chances are you'll stay in that larger home longer than you will in your first home, your investment home. Remember it's best to keep a home for three to five years in order to recoup closing costs.

Avoid any house that's been over-improved, unless the price is in line with other homes in the neighborhood. When sale time rolls around, no one will pay much more than the price at which the other homes are valued.

You should also look for a house that fits into its neighborhood. A Victorian house will be less appealing on a street of split-level ranch houses than it will have on a street with the same 19th-century charm all around it. People who build completely out of keeping with the neighborhood style pay the price.

In this situation, it's best to simply buy an ordinary home and not change things to reflect your personal taste too much. Keep the home plain so that the new buyers can envision their own changes.

WARNING! Many first-time home buyers think their first home is their last. While you may find this surprising, most people stay in their homes an average of only five to seven years. Even if you think you're buying a home for the long term, don't completely write off its resale potential.

Buying for the Long Term

Think of your future family size, entertaining capacity, and your future job on at least a 10-year time frame when looking for your dream home. Listen to your emotions and your gut reaction to the house. You need to like it, really like it, if you're going to live in it for the long haul.

Make sure the house you're considering fits your style and preferences as much as possible. Consider your stage of life. If you have teenagers, will you still need as much room when they're out of the house in five years? Is it really worth moving now? If you are moving to a nice area, particularly a sunny one, you will certainly have friends and family visiting. You may need a guest bedroom or two.

Do you need to take care of aging parents? If you don't have an extra room for this now, perhaps you should check to see if there's enough space on your lot to add another bedroom and bathroom.

Your house will need to change with your life. Check the zoning laws. If you have an extra bedroom and wish to rent it out someday, find out if you are permitted to do so. If you plan to start a business where clients come to your home, you'd better make sure the area is zoned for that.

SCOPING OUT THE NEIGHBORHOODS

Both investment houses and Home Sweet Homes are always better when they sit on the right street. Before you go shopping, take a minute to evaluate the various neighborhoods in your vicinity. The neighborhood is more important than you realize, especially if you're a first-time home buyer. Do you want your house to convey a look of elegance, or does that strike you as pretentious? You'll quickly notice that each neighborhood has its own unique personality. Each tends to attract a certain type of person.

Considerations for Singles

Singles make up a significant portion of the suburban community. Contrary to their traditional image, these comfortable neighborhoods are not just for families. If you are single and considering the suburbs, just make sure there are local activities that interest you so that you can develop a connection to the community.

Considerations for Newlyweds

Think hard about whether this house will be your long-term house or just a starter home intended for resale. Is it the home where you plan to start a family? If you move into a neighborhood where there are other young couples, their next life stage is children. If you move into a neighborhood where the rest of the demographic has teenagers, your children might not have any nearby playmates. Explore the school systems, even if you're not planning on starting a family right away.

Considerations for Families

Bringing children into the equation adds a whole new dimension to house hunting. Now, the neighborhood you pick has to be suitable not only to your needs, but to the needs of everyone else in your household as well. Keep the following issues in the forefront as you search for your new family residence.

• **The Schools:** Probably the first thing on the minds of every parent looking for a new home is the quality of the schools. Even if you get the smallest house in a neighborhood that has outstanding schools, you're ahead of the game. An excellent public school can provide an education comparable to a private school, and you don't have to pay for it. You can get the standardized testing scores for public schools from your state's department of education. Many have websites where they post the test results for each school. Find out how involved parents are in the school. Do they volunteer? Is there an active parent/teacher organization?

• **The Street:** Consider the safety precautions and the speed limits on the street. Look around and see where the children play. If there aren't even enough children nearby, you'll have to arrange play dates elsewhere. Ask your Realtor about the ages of the kids on the street and in the neighborhood. If you're not using a Realtor, ask some of the local parents about the neighborhood. For the best match, try to locate your family in an area that has a demographic similar to your own.

• **Taxes:** In some regions, property is assessed every couple of years, or when the property is sold. Ask your local governing body when the next assessment is due. If you're due for an assessment, the tax rates will be higher than what the seller or even your neighbors are paying. It's important that you know this tax rate in advance of purchase. Lenders will factor in the local tax rate and other factors to determine what mortgage you can afford to pay each month.

WHAT MAKES A HOUSE A DREAM HOME

• **Driving:** While a long commute may seem bearable at first, keep in mind that it will probably become less bearable as the years go by. If you think the new home location will be pushing the limits of your commute tolerance level, think carefully before making the move. The trend where home buyers live far away from their job sites in order to afford a home takes its toll. When the commuting distance reaches fifteen miles or more, the increase in transportation costs start to outweigh the savings gleaned from buying a less expensive home farther away. How long will it take for your children to get to school? How long will it take for your spouse to get to work? These are quality of life questions. Long hours spent commuting may translate into frustration.

• **Activities for Kids:** The easiest way to discover what the neighborhood offers children is to find community websites and/or newsletters. The nearby library should have these resources, or should be able to point you in the right direction. A website and/or newsletter will most likely have school news, development information, activity announcements and other handy details. Find out if there are kids' sports leagues run by volunteers in the neighborhood. Is there an active Girl Scouts and Boy Scouts program? Are there commercial establishments aimed at kids, such as a karate studio or gymnastics facility? Private swim and racquet clubs often offer summer camps and day care programs. These kinds of activities will help both you and your children meet people and develop a solid sense of community.

Considerations for Retirees

If you are close to retirement or have some health concerns, you might want to live close enough to a hospital to ensure your peace of mind. Also, consider if there is public transportation available to the mall, grocery store and social activities so that you can stay mobile and independent. Many neighborhoods have senior centers that can get you involved in activities you might not otherwise have heard about.

SIGNS OF A GOOD NEIGHBORHOOD

• **Stability.** For Sale signs are few and far between.

• **Amenities that add value to the neighborhood.** These include parks with nice playgrounds, sufficient parking, a community center, wide streets with sidewalks, ocean views, tennis courts and a swimming pool. To save money, consider looking at neighborhoods that are on the outskirts of a trendy or high-end neighborhood. You can be close to all the amenities that the high-end neighborhood offers, and your neighborhood is likely to come up in value. Check on what kinds of stores are coming into the area, too.

104   ❖   Home Buying Made Easy

- **Excellent schools.** Even if you don't have school-age children, you still need to be concerned about this aspect. When you get ready to sell your house, families with children will possibly be evaluating your neighborhood. If you want a decent resale value for your home, consider the quality of the schools.

- **Low crime rates.** Call the local police department to get the number of criminal incidents for a particular neighborhood and compare it to other neighborhoods. Many local newspapers also print weekly crime statistics.

- **Pride in ownership.** Drive through the neighborhood and check to see if the lawns, roofs and paint are well-maintained. Weeds taking over and discarded items in the front yards should give you pause. Home values drop in direct proportion to home appearance.

- **Proximity to schools, places of worship, shopping and restaurants.** Make sure these community facilities are here to stay. Notice the demographics they attract. If the community is new, talk to the builders and find out what kinds of shops are coming to the neighborhood.

- **Acceptable street noise.** When touring homes, you may be too preoccupied to notice traffic noise from the street. Visiting in the middle of the day, when traffic is light, will also give you an unrealistic notion of the street noise. Pay attention to the noise levels during peak traffic periods and at night. Traffic noise doesn't blend beautifully into the background like ocean waves crashing onto the beach. Unlike waves, cars don't pass in predictable patterns that the brain eventually gets used to and tunes out. Cars, motorcycles and trucks all have different decibel levels. Your brain never knows what to expect, so it tends to pay attention to each one. A double-yellow line street is a serious concern for parents of young children. While your immediate neighbors may know that kids live nearby, unsuspecting drivers may not register just how slowly they need to drive in residential areas.

DETERMINING COMMUNITY PREFERENCES

After reading the information above, you should be more aware of all the amenities a neighborhood can offer. Try to get as many of them as you can. Use the worksheets at the end of this chapter to prioritize your needs and compare your priorities with those of other family members. You can also use them to compare the neighborhoods side by side if you're not totally sold on one area.

NEW VERSUS EXISTING HOMES

Once you've picked out a neighborhood, the next big decision you have to make is whether a new or an existing home will work best for you. There are advantages and disadvantages to each. In many areas, several home builders get together to create a neighborhood by building twenty or even hundreds of houses on a lot. Along with the houses, they may put in a park, a community center, a playground, a swimming pool and even homes wired with fiber-optic networks. The advantage to this choice is that you get a brand-new home in which you can determine many of the features. Builders give you options on carpeting, tile, wood floors, appliances, countertops and many other features.

The other unique aspect of moving into a band-new community is that everyone there is new. It can become almost like a college dormitory situation where friends are easy to find. With neighbors who are all in the same situation, you'll run into friends at the furniture store, garden shop and hardware store as you all work to get your houses in order. The camaraderie created in a community like this is hard to find in an established neighborhood.

Brand-new communities often have strict homeowners' association rules. You may not be able to have a front porch addition or paint your house in a color that stands out. Think about any dream feature of your house you'll want to add someday and make sure it will be permitted. Go over the homeowners' association rules—and the homeowner's association fees—carefully. Homeowner's association fees can be anywhere from $50 to $500 per month or even more. Make sure you also know how much they're allowed to increase annually.

However, if you enjoy your privacy and appreciate unique architecture, you'll probably find more of those types of perks in an existing community. The following table will help you appreciate the differences between the two choices.

Existing Home versus New Home:

Feature	Existing Home	New Home
Price	Usually less expensive than a comparable new home. All features are already figured into the price, including existing landscaping.	Usually more expensive than comparable existing homes. New home prices also tend to be far less negotiable than existing home prices.
Appearance	It depends. Maybe the former owners kept up the home and made design choices better than you ever could have. Maybe they did not. Either way, you're stuck with what's there.	Not only are the features brand-new, but they were probably added by the builder just for you.
Vegetation	An established neighborhood has more developed trees and bushes, so you know what you're getting. Neighborhoods are usually prettier with more greenery around.	You can choose exactly the vegetation you want around your home (within the limits of the homeowners' association rules).

Feature	Existing Home	New Home
Originality	An existing home is more likely to have more personality, as the owners have added the amenities they liked over the years. If you admire what they've done, you've found your home.	The homes in a new neighborhood may have several different styles, but paint color, roofing, window placement and most other features are very similar.
Space	Ceilings tend to be higher and bedrooms bigger in existing homes.	You may be able to get more overall square footage for your money.
Lot	The yards tend to be larger, and there is more space between homes. They usually require more yard work on the part of the owner.	With space becoming a premium, the houses are being placed on smaller and smaller lots, closer and closer together. The advantage is that there is less yard work to do.
Layout	More original and unique than new homes.	Designed for more efficient traffic flow and better use of space than older homes.
Maintenance	The older home may need more repairs, but the big problems have probably already been worked out. You will learn about all major problems when you go over the disclosure statement with your Realtor.	Every fixture, pipe and appliance is brand-new. If something doesn't function correctly, they are under warranty and can be fixed at no cost.
Environment	Many older homes were not built with the dangers of asbestos, lead paint or other toxic substances taken into consideration.	New homes have to be inspected and must comply with the most current federal, state and local building, fire and environmental codes.
Utility Expenses	Older construction might not have energy efficient features.	The newest homes should have the most energy efficient plumbing, heating and cooling systems.
Interior	The existing home is already decorated. If it's done according to your taste, you don't have to spend time redoing it.	You get to deck the house out according to your taste without having to remove anything.
Extra Expenses	Existing homes tend to have all their schools and community amenities paid for already. Therefore, they do not request homeowner's association fees like the new homes do.	Lower maintenance translates into lower maintenance costs.

COMPARING HOME FEATURES FROM THE INSIDE OUT

The following section covers all of the aspects of a home you will want to consider. Read through them and then take some time to sit down and fill out a few of the helpful worksheets at the end of this chapter. These simple exercises will help you determine what aspects you want, which ones you want more than others and what each member of the family considers a top priority.

WHAT MAKES A HOUSE A DREAM HOME

The View: Don't underestimate the importance of a nice view. Looking out at the ocean, a golf course, a forest or city lights can give you the sense that your home is a peaceful refuge. A great view adds to the resale value of your home. On the other hand, if you are sold on a house with a view, try not to pay for it. Try to keep the price in line with the prices of the other homes on the street. You can even be so bold as to make an offer slightly lower than the market value for another house on the street that doesn't have a view. If the sellers hold firm on their price, you may have to pay for that view if you really want it.

Landscaping: When considering the landscaping, first make sure the irrigation system is in good working order. Determine whether the owner just planted new flowers—flowers that may be prone to dying in a few weeks because the underlying soil has not been properly augmented. Ask whether the flowers have just been planted. The answer is usually yes.

Direction: How the home sits on the lot can affect its appeal. When the sun rises and sets, it warms and lights the home to varying degrees. Make a note about which rooms will have morning and afternoon light. Do you find sunlight streaming in from the kitchen window a welcome sight—but you're not as crazy about sunlight streaming into the bedroom? Try to see if any of the rooms will stay dark for most of the day and gauge whether you can tolerate that.

Heating, Cooling and Water Systems: Do the heating, cooling and water systems meet your preferences? If you like gas, and the home is heated by electricity, it might not be the one for you. What about air conditioning? Is it installed and equipped with central air or wall units? If the home doesn't have air conditioning, is it too cost prohibitive to add it on later? Find out what the utilities bills run. Ask the home seller to show you various utility bills, and then do your research. Find out what the usual cost is for running the heat or air conditioning in the neighborhood. A quick call to the local utility companies should provide that answer. If you are buying a new home, the builder should have a general idea about what the heating and air conditioning bills will be. Are the heating, cooling and water systems functioning properly, and are they energy efficient? What is the SEER rating (Seasonal Energy Efficiency Ratio)? This unit of measure indicates the performance efficiency of the system. The higher the SEER rating, the more efficient the unit is.

Construction Material: Brick and stone homes are usually considered upscale and desirable. Wood is also at the top of the list, except in areas where termites can cause a lot of trouble. While vinyl or aluminum siding may save you maintenance time and money, it will not add to the resale value of the house. Buyers in the Southwest have pretty much resigned themselves to stucco, but in the North, where the weather can crack the surface, it is considered neither attractive nor practical.

Driveway: Most buyers prefer blacktop and concrete driveways. Kids play better there than on gravel. In fact, a gravel driveway is usually considered a drawback to the house.

Pool/Jacuzzi: While the pool may seem sparkling and peaceful when you tour the home, it requires considerable upkeep. Also, a pool can be a safety hazard for young children. You'll need to take necessary precautions so that the pool area stays safe. Consult the local authorities for safety guidance.

Windows: Much of your heating and cooling bill could be affected by the home's windows. Self-insulating windows and sliding glass doors are definite selling points for a home. Storm windows are as well. Even in hot climates, well-insulated windows are necessary for keeping the cool air inside.

Kitchen: The kitchen is the heart of the home. The most intimate conversations take place here, and a lot of love is dispensed from the oven. Many home buyers want both a dining room and an eat-in kitchen. Watch out for water under the sink. This could indicate leaking fixtures or pipes. Make sure the home inspector gets a good look at this area.

Family Room: Some rooms of the house are not as necessary as in prior eras. In the 1950s, the prevalent, formal cocktail parties made living rooms a must. Now that alcohol is not necessarily present at most parties, entertaining is getting more casual. A living room is not considered absolutely necessary. Many sit unused a great deal of the time. Instead, builders in the South and West have been combining the kitchen, eating area and family room into one "great room" with no walls dividing them. Buyers respond well to this design idea. The day of the formal living room has passed. These days, people are cooking, eating and playing all at once. That's why the great room has caught on so well. Find out if there are cable outlets for an Internet hookup in case you want to use the family room as an office. Keeping the office by the kitchen puts the two most potentially disorganized and cluttered places in the same area. If you go this route, the rest of the home will stay neat and ready for entertaining.

Dining Room: Like the living room, the dining room may soon be going the way of the dinosaur. While some may want a large, formal dining room, many prefer an eat-in kitchen. If you do have a formal dining room, you'll need a door right to the kitchen. Having it separated from the kitchen by a hallway or staircase is inconvenient and will not go over well with buyers when you go to sell the home.

Master Bedroom: This room is often considered a refuge for the adults. We'd all like a nice large one—a little apartment away from it all. Pay attention to where and when the sun comes in the windows. Morning sun can wake you up too early. Afternoon sun can make the room very hot for sleeping at night. You can fix both problems with insulated "black out" shades or curtains. These are inexpensive items that are easy to install.

Other Bedrooms: While the biggest bedroom in the home is usually the master, the other bedrooms can be just as appealing with creative decorating and furniture arrangements. Use smaller scale furniture in small rooms and keep the room as clutter-free as possible. Have one centerpiece in a room and coordinate the rest of the items with it. Small patterns or even solid colors on textured fabrics help small rooms feel larger. It's always good to have a guest room on a different level than the family bedrooms. This provides both hosts and guests with a little privacy and space.

Bathrooms: Bathrooms take third place behind kitchens and bedrooms when it comes to rooms that factor highly in home selection. The general rule for bathrooms is the more the better. A moisture vent is a good feature to have in all bathrooms. In fact, some building codes and home loans require it. Find out how strong the water pressure is. High water pressure can take its toll on the home's pipes. If the home experienced a pipe leak or break, be extra cautious.

Attic: The best attics come with older homes. While they're not usually livable because of sloping ceilings, they can make fun play spaces for young kids (if adequately ventilated), and they make good storage space. Most homes have attics, but whether or not they're genuinely accessible is another story. Keep in mind that an attic that is not properly ventilated can range between the two extremes of 100 degrees and -30 degrees. The things you decide to store may not tolerate such swings in temperature.

Basement: Believe it or not, the basement is a very important aspect of a home. Basements are found most often in the North and the Midwest. They can add up to 50 percent more room to a two-story home and 100 percent more space to a ranch home. Basements add to the resale value of your home. Watch for mold and mildew, as well as any evidence of water leaks.

Garage: A garage can do a lot more than just store your car. Most homeowners don't utilize this space efficiently. When you're touring a home, make sure the garage meets your needs. A finished garage is preferred over an unfinished one. Finished garages usually have insulation and built-in shelving. Insulation keeps the garage cooler in the summer and warmer in the winter. If you have a workshop in your garage (or even a home office) you'll appreciate the insulation. It's even important that the garage door be insulated. An insulated door can make a big difference in temperature control.

Overall Traffic Flow: Builders of brand-new homes are happy to give you copies of floor plans. While owners of older homes usually don't provide this convenience, you can always map it out yourself on the grid included in this book.

ASSESSING FUTURE HOME NEEDS NOW

Considering personal preferences is an important part of the home buying process and one that can feel overwhelming at times. To help you get these aspects all sorted out, take the time to fill out the worksheets provided in this book. It's also worth your time to put some thought into what you think you will need five to fifteen years in the future. You'll save money on closing and moving costs by finding the right house now that will suit you for a long time. What typically causes the biggest shift in housing needs are changes to the family structure and aging. The worksheets at the end of this chapter will help you make the right decision. Remember, even a dream home has to have practical features. Knowing what you want and need now and in the future—before you go on that first tour—will help you make a sound judgment.

NEIGHBORHOOD PRIORITIES WORKSHEET

Use this worksheet to rate the neighborhoods you visit on a scale of 1 to 10 (10 being the best). Then add the numbers at the bottom of the table. The neighborhood with the highest score is the right neighborhood for you and your family.

	Neighborhood #1	Neighborhood #2	Neighborhood #3
Neighborhood name			
Resale value			
Schools			
Commute time			
Proximity to shopping			
Availability of adults' activities			
Availability of kids' activities			
Kids in the neighborhood			
Availability of public transportation			
Neighborhood demographics			
Neighborhood style			
Neighborhood upkeep			
Crime rate			
Vegetation			
Zoning (for a renter or to start a home business, for example)			
Community activities			
TOTAL SCORE:			

When you find a house you like, answer the following questions to gauge whether or not it will work for you in five years, ten years and fifteen years.

Space Considerations	In 5 Years	In 10 Years	In 15 Years
How many bedrooms will you need?			
Will you need another bathroom?			
Will you need a home office?			
Will you have enough storage space?			
Will you need to build an addition?			
Will you need a larger yard for children?			
How many cars will you have?			
Will the driveway be big enough?			
Will the garage be large enough?			
Will you need to finish off a basement or attic for more room?			
Will you have enough room for pets?			
Other:			

Aging Considerations	In 5 Years	In 10 Years	In 15 Years
How many stories will you need/want?			
How much yard work will you want to do or be able to do?			
Will you want to be able to walk to shops and activities?			
Other:			

DREAM HOME WISH LIST WORKSHEET

Use the following two worksheets to determine which features in a house are important to you and your family. If you are filling this out with your partner, consider using two different colors of ink so it will be clear who prefers what.

Rooms	Definitely	Would Be Nice	Don't Need
Large Kitchen			
Formal Dining Room			
Family Room			
Finished Basement			
Unfinished Basement			
Finished Garage			
Unfinished Garage			
Attic			
Workout Room			
Home Office			
Screened Porch			
Play/Bonus Room			
Laundry Room			

Amenities	Definitely	Would Be Nice	Don't Need
Big Closets			
Fireplace			
Central Air			
Built-in Cabinets			
Deck			
Swimming Pool			
Jacuzzi			
Smart House			
Forced Air Heat			
Gas/Radiator Heat			

General Interior	Definitely	Would Be Nice	Don't Need
Perfect Condition			
Fixer-upper			
Hardwood Floors			
Carpeting			
Light and Bright			
Dark and Cozy			
Lots of Storage			
Appealing Paint Color			
Appealing Window Coverings			

Exterior	Definitely	Would Be Nice	Don't Need
Perfect Condition			
Fixer-upper			
Curb Appeal			
View			
Electric Outlets Front & Rear			
Water Faucets Front & Rear			
Big Yard			
Small Yard			
Paved Driveway			
Upscale Landscaping			
Room for Garden			
Room for Home Addition			
Custom Landscaping			
Fenced Yard			
Dog Run			
Storm Windows			

The following four worksheets allow you to record comments regarding the various features and rooms of the houses you visit. You can compare up to eight homes. If you need more, feel free to make copies of these worksheets.

Feature	House 1	House 2	House 3	House 4
Address				
City				
Realtor				
Phone				
Email				
Listing Price				
Square Footage				
Size of lot				
Months in the market				
Convenient to schools?				
Convenient to work?				
Homeowners' Association Fees				
Age of Home				
Number of Bedrooms				
Number of Bathrooms				
Number of Stories				
Curb Appeal				
General Exterior Condition				
View				
Backyard				
Front Yard				
Garage				
Windows				
Laundry Room				

Feature	House 1	House 2	House 3	House 4
Describe Floor Plan				
Describe Kitchen				
Describe Family Room				
Describe Dining Room				
Describe Living Room				
Describe Master Bedroom				
Describe Master Bath				
Describe Bedroom 1				
Describe Bedroom 2				
Describe Bedroom 3				
Describe Bedroom 4				
Describe Office				
Describe Garage				
Other				
Other				
Other				
Other				
Other				
Other				

Feature	House 5	House 6	House 7	House 8
Address				
City				
Realtor				
Phone				
Email				
Listing Price				
Square Footage				
Size of lot				
Months in the market				
Convenient to schools?				
Convenient to work?				
Homeowners' Association Fees				
Age of Home				
Number of Bedrooms				
Number of Bathrooms				
Number of Stories				
Curb Appeal				
General Exterior Condition				
View				
Backyard				
Front Yard				
Garage				
Windows				
Laundry Room				

Feature	House 5	House 6	House 7	House 8
Describe Floor Plan				
Describe Kitchen				
Describe Family Room				
Describe Dinning Room				
Describe Living Room				
Describe Master Bedroom				
Describe Master Bath				
Describe Bedroom 1				
Describe Bedroom 2				
Describe Bedroom 3				
Describe Bedroom 4				
Describe Office				
Describe Garage				
Other				
Other				
Other				
Other				
Other				
Other				

ROOM DIMENSIONS WORKSHEET

This worksheet allows you to compare the size of the rooms of the various houses you are considering.

House Layout	House 1	House 2	House 3	House 4	House 5	House 6	House 7	House 8
Dining room size								
Kitchen size								
Family room size								
Living room size								
Den/Office size								
Bedroom #1 size								
Bedroom #2 size								
Bedroom #3 size								
Bedroom #4 size								
Bathroom #1 size								
Bathroom #2 size								
Additional room size								
Additional room size								
Additional Room Size								
Additional Room Size								
Garage size								

BUYING A CONDOMINIUM

For many home buyers, a condominium is the entrance ramp to real estate ownership. And a fine entrance ramp it is. Escaping your rental via the condominium route is a winning financial strategy. In recent years, condominiums have become hot commodities for retirees looking for a simpler lifestyle. This demographic shift has caused condominium prices to increase faster in the last few years than prices on single family homes in most areas. While typically one out of five home buyers acquires a condominium, look for that figure to increase in the coming years as more and more Baby Boomers retire and scale down.

Condominiums can be a great solution for those who want to avoid home maintenance hassles and for those who want to live in certain affluent areas, perhaps close to cities where detached homes are few and far between.

The word "condominium" is derived from two Latin roots: "con" or "with" and "dominion" or "ownership." The underlying meaning comes from owning (having dominion over) a property, with others. A condo doesn't necessarily have to be part of a 20-story high-rise. It can be half of a townhome or one or two rooms in a larger divided home. The most important concept you must grasp now is that once you buy a condominium, you automatically become a member of the community's homeowners' association, as you own in common with others.

The greatest advantage to owning a condo is that you can get more space for your money. You will get your forced savings program (your home equity will build), and you have the long-term security and freedom to do almost whatever you want with the inside of your property.

FINANCIAL ADVANTAGES AND DISADVANTAGES

Many home buyers don't realize that when they buy a condo, they not only own the area between the walls they'll live in, but also a portion of:

- the land under the complex
- exterior building walls
- garage
- lobby
- swimming pool
- meeting room

- the roof
- basement
- elevators
- hallways
- tennis courts

You own them "in common" with other owners. These are amenities you benefit from, but they are also your responsibility. An owner of a detached home usually doesn't have these extra common grounds. Imagine the legal red tape and financial wrangling that accompanies each. To make things easier, all homeowners of the condominium are united under the homeowners' association. Some of the owners choose to be very involved; others just wait for the meeting minutes to show up in their mailbox. There are often enough people to fill the board if administrative meetings are not your thing. The association has a budget, balance sheets and financial documents that have to be looked over by an accountant.

When you buy a condo, you will be given a percentage of the joint ownership of the complex. That percentage determines just how high your dues are. Those with the larger, more luxurious condominiums are usually assessed more fees. Regular monthly dues aren't the only expenses with condominium ownership. "Special assessments" are additional dues that may be required from everyone when a large expense needs to be covered or an emergency occurs. While special assessments sound daunting, they can also be an advantage. If the heating system breaks down, the owner of the detached residence is in for thousands of dollars in repair fees and new equipment. The condo owner needs to pay only a portion of those costs. While the heating system for a condominium building is far more expensive than that of a detached home, with scores of owners paying for that large expense, every individual's portion is quite reasonable.

When purchasing a condo, make sure you understand the three most important documents: the Master Deed (otherwise known as the Declaration of Covenants, Conditions and Restrictions), the homeowners' association bylaws and the homeowners' association budget. If you have any questions about these documents, ask the home-owners' association for clarification or contact a real estate attorney.

What's Considered Outrageous in the CC&Rs?

When so many people live so close to each other, it's reasonable to use mutually agreed upon rules to keep order and maintain happiness for the majority. You may consider your CC&Rs overly restrictive if they dictate:

- style of floor and wall coverings
- if you can or cannot sublet
- whether or not you can make improvements inside your unit
- when and how often you can entertain
- type and number of pets you can have

Red Flags in a Homeowners' Association Budget

No one likes to face big debts coming due down the road. Look for the following financial issues:

- Operating expenses climbing higher year by year so that the next year they will overwhelm the association's budget. If so, you can count on fees being raised pretty quickly.

- 3-5 percent of the complex's operating budget should be available in cash reserves for emergencies and predictable major expenses such as repaving the parking lot.

- Poor fiscal management can be found in the past several years' operating budgets and financial statements. Look for frequent, significant dues increases. Dues increases should not be too far ahead of the current rate of inflation.

- Too many homeowners who are late paying their dues. This could indicate dissatisfaction with the board, or it could indicate uninvolved tenants. You don't want either in the complex you choose.

CONSIDERATIONS FOR DIFFERENT LIFE STAGES:

- **Singles**
  Condominium ownership benefits this group the most. (Retirees are a close second.) Despite the homeowners' association fees, since the costs of exterior maintenance is split by everyone, you will end up paying less than you would if, for example, you had to replace the whole roof of a detached home yourself. A plumbing leak in your unit is taken care of by the group, as is the exterior paint job. When something goes wrong with the condominium's exterior, the association officers are right on it. They have the maintenance people lined up.

BUYING A CONDOMINIUM

You also have an advantage when something goes wrong in your unit. Chances are the board members have reliable contractors, plumbers and electricians to recommend. Finally, the grounds are taken care of by people who have actually operated lawn mowers and leaf blowers, so that's another obligation off your plate. The condominium lifestyle suits singles well. There are often more condominiums than detached residences located near urban areas. Singles can be close to work and the nightlife that helps them meet friends and even a potential spouse. The condominium complex lends itself to meeting others if it's small or medium sized. Residents meet neighbors and potential friends at the pools, recreation centers and tennis courts in condominium complexes. On your own, you most likely wouldn't be able to afford all of these extras. With its costs split between you and your neighbors, a comfortable life is not out of reach.

One possible drawback for those young and just starting out is that if you don't pay your home association fees, the association puts a lien on your property. These fines could eat up whatever equity you are able to build in the early years.

- **Newlyweds**
Condominiums are also a great option for newlyweds, particularly if you find one in a neighborhood where you can raise your family. You can start getting to know the area and its shops, community centers and parks before you consider having children.

A condo could be a good way for you and your spouse to save money. It would be smart to get a mortgage lower than what the bank will actually approve so that you can build up your IRAs at work.

- **Families**
While it's not the home with the white picket fence, a condominium could be a good solution for many families. A condominium usually runs 20 to 30 percent less than a detached home for the same amount of square footage. If you need extra bedrooms to separate siblings who need their own space, the condo could be the way to go.

The big drawback for families when it comes to condos is the lack of privacy. Your neighbors (who will be sharing your walls, floors and ceilings) hear your noise, and you hear theirs. If your children are even loud when playing, you could be the subject of complaints and brought up before the homeowners' association. You can tell them you'll work to quiet the kids all you want, but kids are kids, and kids yell, jump from furniture and run down long hallways. Do you have the emotional and mental resources to keep their boundless energies in check?

To build on this, if you have a new baby and sleep is paramount, the noise in a condominium complex could disturb both your few stolen hours of sleep and the baby's. If condo noise makes it harder to get the baby on a reliable nap schedule, the whole family routine could be disrupted.

Most families find a yard, even a small one, crucial for family harmony. Even one swing, one sandbox or one little dog can help dispense children's energy. Yards also provide areas for pretend and an escape from parents into a safe imaginary world. Children do appreciate the natural world, and many spend hours outside exploring the insect and plant life thriving there.

- **Retirees**
Those looking to scale down from a larger family home appreciate the simpler, easier lifestyle the condominium offers.

At the condominium complex, lawn and exterior maintenance are taken care of by others. This fact is more important to retirees than to singles, because retirees may be less capable physically of taking care of large outdoor tasks. Since many complexes have service personnel, it's easier to make arrangements when traveling for mail pickup or plant watering. Convenience isn't the only advantage of condominium life. Like singles, if retirees pick the right complex (and the right size), they too can find others with similar interests and activities. There are meeting rooms for card games, family parties and club get-togethers, pools for exercise and Jacuzzis for relaxation. Since there are more condominiums than detached homes in most urban areas, retirees who choose this option often find that they can walk to the grocery store, the library, the movies and many other shops.

With home maintenance costs shared, individual owners can save more. Seniors on fixed incomes usually appreciate that while they essentially have to chip in $100 for the downstairs neighbor's pipe leak, all the neighbors chip in $100 when their air conditioning system ceases to function. Air conditioning repairs can cost thousands of dollars. Those on fixed incomes usually budget every last dollar. The big unexpected expenses can really throw them for a loop. While home maintenance issues do arise with the same frequency as they do with detached homes, at least retirees can depend on a steady, reasonable monthly cash outflow rather than having to cash out a huge chunk of their investment portfolio from which they draw income.

The biggest drawback to condominium life for seniors is the fact that they have to go by certain rules. Another caution for seniors involves noise and privacy. Walls can be thin, and the long hallways lined with doors can amplify every noise. If you're looking forward to much-deserved peace and quiet, you need to hang out at the complex at different times of the day in order to know just what the traffic will be. Don't necessarily trust the testimony of whoever's showing you the condo. Your noise tolerance levels may differ from theirs.

TIPS FOR EXPLORING CONDOMINIUMS

Since you're basically combining funds with the other owners, there are some things you should be aware of when touring condominiums and analyzing their balance sheets. Also, since you're going to be pretty close to neighbors, you'll want to make sure you can tolerate each other.

Meet with the condominium's board members. When you get together, try to pick up on the values and priorities of the people who live in the complex. The board members often reflect the overall philosophy of the owners. Ask if you can speak to an owner or two. This is not unreasonable.

Make sure to ask about major improvements on the horizon and whether those major improvements will require a special assessment. Ask about other repairs that are either underway or coming up soon to get an idea of the soundness of the condominium.

Find out how many tenants are renting and how many own their properties. If owners are the vast majority, the community will be more cohesive and will probably take better care of the grounds and each unit.

Ask whether there is a reserve of cash from which the association can draw in case of an emergency.

Board members are used to answering questions like these. Consider writing your questions down and going through them one by one with the condominium's representative.

Remember that detached homes are not the only way to get the feeling of "mine all mine" in a home. There are many advantages to owning a condominium, should your finances and lifestyle mesh. Condos can give you the same square footage at a discount of 20 to 30 percent, compared to detached homes. They have amenities that an owner of a detached home probably couldn't afford or even have the square footage to provide. On the other hand, condos can be legally and financially complicated.

EVALUATING CONDOMINIUMS WORKSHEET

Use the following four worksheets to compare the various condominiums that you visit. You can compare up to five condominiums. If you need more, feel free to make copies of these worksheets.

Attributes	Condominium #1	Condominium #2
Age of the complex		
Number of units in the complex		
Address		
Size in square feet		
Number of bedrooms		
Number of bathrooms		
Number of stories		
Are there units above or below?		
Describe setup		
How is the view?		
Percentage of owner occupied		
Percentage of tenant occupied		
Amount of homeowners' association fees		
Who manages the homeowners' association?		
How much does the homeowners' association have in reserve?		
Are there any current or past litigations?		
Are the CC&Rs satisfactory or too restrictive?		
Are the bylaws agreeable? If not, why?		
Can you have pets?		
Can you rent out your unit?		
Does the condo community have a good reputation?		
Does the condo association management have a good reputation?		
What common grounds are included?		
What is the condition of the grounds?		
Is the community well maintained?		

Condominium #3	Condominium #4	Condominium #5

Attributes	Condominium #1	Condominium #2
Does the unit come with a garage or parking space? If so, how many cars will it fit?		
Is there adequate guest parking?		
Is there storage on the premises?		
How many units are for sale now?		
How long have they been on the market? What is typical in this complex?		
Do owners like the community? What positives and negatives do they say?		
How long have most owners lived there?		
Do you like the process of the meetings and have you reviewed past meeting notes?		
Additional notes.		

Condo Layout

Dining room size:		
Kitchen size:		
Family room size:		
Living room size:		
Den/Office size:		
Bedroom #1 size:		
Bedroom #2 size:		
Bedroom #3 size:		
Bathroom #1 size::		
Bathroom #2 size:		
Additional room size:		
Additional room size:		
Additional room size:		
Garage size:		

Condominium #3	Condominium #4	Condominium #5

NOTES

TIPS ON GETTING
A GOOD DEAL

Most people relish getting a bargain. In retail stores, we're used to discounts up to 50 percent and sometimes even 75 percent off. Discounts of this magnitude don't occur in the real estate market. In fact—brace yourself—the average buyer usually gets only 6 percent off the asking price for a home. That may not sound like much, but houses have always been American's best investment. Paying for a $650,000 house in a market where the range is $475,000 to $575,000 may seem unwise and/or naïve. In 15 years, when the home you bought is valued far above even the $650,000 figure, you won't even remember that you were put off by that initial price.

WARNING! Real estate "get rich quick" schemes flicker after the late night and weekend shows. They can bankrupt you faster than you can say "multimillionaire." The promoters claim that you can easily buy property on which a seller has defaulted for great savings. They even try to build up the advantages of buying condemned property.

Don't get saddled with a property that has incurable faults. A deteriorating location, no backyard, an unreachable water leak or a cracked slab are defects that no amount of money can repair. Forgo spending money on the books and videotapes these schemes hawk, particularly if you have little or no experience in real estate. If those people are making so much money in real estate, why are they wasting their precious time trying to sell you their program in the form of books and CDs? They could be out there snapping up condemned properties and dilapidated foreclosures!

COMMON SENSE DEALS

Getting a deal on a home is much harder than finding a bargain on a new car or pair of jeans. But there are some circumstances where it's possible to keep tens of thousands of your hard earned dollars. A 6 percent reduction in housing price is the norm. Under the right circumstances, you might be able to get a significantly greater reduction.

In home selling, there is such a thing as seller desperation. Have you ever seen a home advertised with the words "motivated seller?" Sellers get motivated for many reasons. The primary one is that their house is not selling. If a home has been listed in the MLS for 60 days, you can be certain the seller is getting skittish. You can feel confident making a low offer. A home price reduction is another indication of desperation on the part of the seller.

Another trick is to find out the circumstances behind the move, if you can. This is where a Realtor comes in handy. The Realtor can probably get more information from the seller's Realtor than you can get from the seller. If the seller has already bought a new home, or if he or she is divorcing or transferring because of a job change, the pressure to sell quickly intensifies. With these conditions present, a low offer is not unexpected. It may even be appreciated.

BUY A FIXER-UPPER

During your tour of homes, you will probably come across one or two where neither the seller nor the agent seems to care how the place looks. Chipped and scratched paint, stained carpeting, heavy window coverings, outdated appliances, dull cabinets and scuffed floors can all be taken care of at a reasonable cost with minimal effort. Try to look past that stained avocado carpeting to an image of yourself handing wads of saved cash over to the hardwood floor installer. A dingy, shabby house will give you a bad feeling immediately. Try to fight the emotion and see the house for more important things like room size, location and layout. Windows can be built into walls in a dark home; appliances can be upgraded in a 1970s-era kitchen.

If you're still unsure, consider hiring an appraiser to give you an idea about the house's value. Usually, an appraiser comes on the scene only when an offer is made and accepted. The appraiser reassures the bank that the price agreed upon is within a reasonable range. (So that if you default on your loan, the bank can sell your house and fully recoup its investment.) In this case, getting an appraisal before making an offer can be a smart move. If a house like this is the shabbiest on a street of well-kept homes, think hard before passing it by. Cosmetic adjustments can change the look of a place tremendously. In a neighborhood on the rise, these changes add great value to your home. Some homeowners just don't know what they have right in their hands.

Before you imagine yourself bragging to your friends about your great deal, keep in mind that it takes time to coordinate the repair work. You will have to compare prices and the work of different contractors, negotiate for their best prices and even oversee their efforts. That doesn't mean you have to figure it all out yourself. For guidance and other helpful ideas on giving an existing home a makeover, we suggest referring to another excellent book in this series, *Home Improvement Made Easy*.

THE DOWNSIDE OF FIXER-UPPERS

The cosmetic changes mentioned above may be easy to pull off, but some homes have drastic repairs and remodeling to be done. If you have the gift of seeing beyond the ugly duckling to the beautiful swan, a fixer-upper could be the house for you. In slow real estate markets, prices are low enough that homes in great condition are affordable. But if you're in a seller's market and you just can't get into that pristine home, the fixer-upper might be a good option. The drawback is that you have to have enough cash after the real estate transaction to make the home livable. The best people for fixers are those who are good at home repair and decoration or at least interested in both. You can add thousands of dollars of value to your home by installing a better bathroom, upgrading the kitchen or adding canned lighting throughout the house. Some people actually find these tasks to be a relaxing hobby.

If you remember that you only have to refurbish one room at a time, some of the pressure dissipates. The whole house doesn't have to be renovated all at once. Pace yourself so you don't get burned out. Great satisfaction will come from knowing that you've made the house yours, room by room, wall by wall, corner by corner. Also, you will be able to decorate the house from the bottom up in your own unique style.

Some fixer-uppers are easier to transform than others. Ugly, peeling paint can be stripped off in days, and anyone can learn how to prime and paint walls, railings and ceilings. The folks at the home maintenance stores are happy to help. Repairing shutters and window treatments are also child's play. You get into deeper waters with a fixer-upper when your Cinderella home has a cracked slab or lacks a master bedroom, garage or functioning plumbing system. These kinds of upgrades run into the tens of thousands of dollars.

If you decide to bid on a fixer-upper, get a fit and fastidious home inspector. He/she will need to catalogue every deficiency. Get the inspection done before you make your offer. With a list of needed repairs, you'll know exactly the financial, time and energy expenditure required if you decide to buy the home. More importantly, the seller will also realize this and may be more willing to meet your low offer.

It's smart to get both the appraisal and the inspection done before you put together your offer. This is not unheard of in the real estate business, and the seller (or at least the seller's agent) will not take offense. You can also bring contractors along and ask for quotes on projected jobs. Use these bids to negotiate a better offer. Keep in mind, however, that organizing this team will take time and effort. Realistically evaluate whether you have either. Remember to check each contractor with the Better Business Bureau or review references thoroughly.

TIPS ON GETTING A GOOD DEAL

BUY IN A GLOOMY ECONOMY

Economies rise and fall. When unemployment is high and consumer confidence low, it sometimes seems that the paradigm has shifted, that the good times are over and a new, harsh reality has taken its place. Since most people ignore the media when it reports positive news, down times are a gold mine for all newspapers and news shows. People sit rapt watching for signs of a turn of events, but a somber faced newscaster delivers yet more frightening statistics and findings about the eventual downfall of American dominance. The media's predictions further convince us that we are sliding into certain poverty. People become afraid to change jobs, buy products or move. Housing prices plummet. Media-fueled negativity serves one entity the very best: news outlets. And luckily for us, its predictions are usually only temporary. Reporters eventually get bored with their own monotonous warnings and move onto other stories. The Federal Reserve and other government bodies have placed controls on the economy since the great stock market crash of 1929. This protects us from entering a depression of the magnitude of the 1930s. While conflicts do rage across the world, war actually helps economies by creating jobs. The global economy is slowly lifting the fortunes of those in many third world countries and over time making them consumers of first world products. The long-term prognosis for the American housing market is a steady increase in altitude with some expected turbulence.

Are you still leery? Maybe you're just young. When you're in your 20s or early 30s, it's harder to stomach buying in a down market. You haven't seen housing markets and the economy ride through their cycles, but they do. Try to find the positive news in the economy and focus on that. Get opinions from your elders and remember, like the famous saying goes, "courage is not the absence of fear, but fear with the addition of action." In fact, the presence of fear is necessary for one to be courageous.

BUY DURING WINTER

Excitement for new homes blossoms in the Springtime. Parents want to buy a new house in the spring so that they can move in the summer while the kids are between school years. Real estate markets in all areas have their busy season from March or April through the early summer when lots of buyers are out looking.

If you can hold off house-hunting until the three weeks between Thanksgiving and Christmas, you may just find a bargain. Chances are the house tours will be pretty empty. Winter in general is the slow time for moving real estate, and the colder your region, the longer the slow housing market lasts. In the Northwest, potential home buyers head out after March. In the South, spring hits in mid-February.

Winter isn't the only slow period. In some areas, the market often slows down in July and August, at the peak of summer vacation season. This slowdown is not as drastic as in the cold months. Slow periods are the most conducive to making low offers.

WARNING! Keep in mind that the homes available during these times may be unwanted leftovers.

LOWBALL YOUR OFFER

If you are not necessarily looking for your dream home, you may consider making "lowball" offers. Be ready to lose the home and even risk offending the seller. A lowball offer is generally 20 to 25 percent lower than the asking price or fair market value. This strategy is appropriate if you're buying the home as an investment property or you're single and just want to get into a house, any house. You don't expect to become attached to the house. It's often a condo or townhome you might own before finding your spouse. Your bachelor/bachelorette pad could be a potential down payment generator if you're successful in your bid.

If you adopt a lowball strategy, you may make twenty offers on twenty different homes and get just one counteroffer and nineteen offended sellers. Take heart, those you've offended you'll probably never see again, and the inexpensive house will pad your nest egg.

If you fall in love with the house, however, don't even consider a lowball offer. Homes are very tied to emotions, and an owner may become deeply insulted. If it is your dream home, you'll be in it for many years if not decades.

CONSIDER THE UNPROVEN NEIGHBORHOODS

New neighborhoods may strike you as unproven, but there are ways you can get a good deal if you do a little research. Luckily, you don't have to do your own market research. Plenty of folks from other organizations have done that already. What you need to do is scout the area for promising growth by looking for the construction of new homes, malls and schools. If you see a mall going up, find out what kinds of shops have leased space. If they are upscale retailers, it's clear that those businesses view the incipient neighborhood as attracting that kind of clientele. If you read the newspaper or neighborhood circulars, you can probably find the phone number of the neighborhood's planning committee. The folks there will be well aware of what businesses have expressed interest in opening up shop in that area.

While scouting the neighborhood, keep in mind that the older homes there have a better value than a brand-new home getting the finishing touches from a builder. There is less competition and fewer buyers for the older homes. And older is relative! In Massachusetts, it might mean a 300-year-old home, while in Los Angeles it could be a home built 35 years ago.

LOOK INTO FORECLOSURES

In recent years, there has been an uptick in the number of foreclosures on homes. This is mostly due to fancy financing (namely balloon and piggyback loans) that get people into homes but have a high price to pay five years down the road. In California, mortgage defaults doubled in 2006 for Riverside and San Diego counties and in Northern California in general. They increased by over 80 percent in Orange and Ventura counties and in the state's Central Valley area.

What if you have to foreclose?
If foreclosure looms on your horizon, keep in mind that you can negotiate a "workout" with your lender to pay what is past due over time. If that fails, owners can make a deal where they sell their property to the bank for less than the loan amount with no extra balance. Homeowners can also turn to their federal and state governments to see if they qualify for some debt bailout programs.

Homeowners got caught up in—as former Federal Reserve Chairman Alan Greenspan put it— "irrational exuberance" and overbought during the real estate run-up in the first five years of the millennium. Some people who buy foreclosures below their appraised values do indeed get lucky. If you're considering this strategy, talk to an appraiser first and have them ready to move when a foreclosure becomes available. Be ready to go to any neighborhood. Foreclosures are often not as sweet a deal as you would think.

The owner is now the very savvy lender or bank. He or she knows just what the comparable home values are. The bank only discounts their price so much for the convenience of having a problem property taken off their hands. They can be savvy, stubborn and smart negotiators.

Let's say you do get a good price on a foreclosure. Just what have you acquired along with the keys? Some homeowners are so distraught at going into foreclosure that they destroy the property. Did we mention that many lenders don't let you do a home inspection before you bid on the property? This is why. Angry former homeowners may tear out the sinks, the cabinets, the toilets and anything else they think they may be able to use later. Do you really want a property that you can't inspect before buying?

Keep in mind that getting a foreclosure property can take anywhere from a few months to more than a year to complete. Beware of sellers who begin to sell the property after just being notified that their lender is going to foreclose on them. These types could lie about unrecorded mortgages on the house, tax liens and property tax liens. These debts will be yours once you get title on the house. In the eyes of the law, the house owes the money and whoever owns the house is responsible for its debt. The lien is against the house.

The last frightening scenario involving a foreclosure is the image of the moving truck rolling up outside your new home only to find the previous "owner" still there in their bathrobe with nary a box packed. Eviction takes several months.

Only look at foreclosures being offered by lenders. The lenders are required by law to do a title search and find all the tax liens and second mortgages associated with the home. To find these foreclosures, go to your local real estate office, preferably a discount real estate office, if you really want to save money. These companies have lists of foreclosures. You can also go to your local Housing and Urban Development (HUD) office. Sometimes, banks will post lists of their foreclosures. Call their mortgage departments to get this list. You'll often find, however, that the mortgage officers will send you to a Realtor or HUD.

If you have a good down payment, you may be able to convince the lender to let you inspect the home. Some lenders will agree to this, but the majority of them will not. Finally, work to get a loan at an interest rate lower than market from the lender. You may get lucky and work a deal with no down payment, a reduced interest rate and/or lower escrow fees. The bank doesn't want to manage property. It wants to buy and sell money in the form of loans.

Probably the ideal candidate to buy a foreclosure is someone who already has a home to live in and is looking for investment properties. This person will also be adept at home repair. Finally, this person should be savvy enough to understand the subtleties of loans, the legal issues surrounding title and the condition of the foreclosed property. Since this is not the typical home buyer, we encourage the majority of you to stay away from foreclosures!

NOTES

CHOOSING A REALTOR

Now that you know so much about the intricacies of home financing, the housing market and home amenities, you may think you do not need an agent. And you may be right.

In the last decade, "For Sale by Owner" signs have proliferated. If you're selling in California, Boston, New York City or Washington, D.C., (where you can't get a decent detached home for less than $500,000), the seller needs to pay a 6 percent commission on the sale price, or in this case $30,000. That's a big chunk of the seller's profit. It's clear why a seller would want to sell on his/her own. But why would a buyer try to enter this kind of transaction without the support of a real estate agent?

There are several reasons why buyers may consider For Sale by Owner homes. On rare occasions, a house purchase may be agreed upon between two private parties. Friends or acquaintances may help each other out by agreeing to buy a home. In these instances, buyers aren't touring multiple houses or getting information about different streets and neighborhoods. The real estate agent only needs to put the right papers in front of the right person and gather signatures. A real estate lawyer can provide this service for around $500.

Another common scenario wherein a buyer's agent is not advisable is when a For Sale by Owner seller makes it clear he/she will not work with a buyer's agent. If you find exactly the right house on exactly the right street, but a curmudgeon lives there—you will have to play ball by his or her rules. Don't let this insistence cause panic.

This seller is probably a do-it-yourselfer who has researched how to conduct a real estate transaction legally and without liability on his or her part. For peace of mind, you can hire a real estate attorney for a reasonable price (again, around $500) to go over all of the documents provided by the seller. Call around to several attorneys. Tell them what is involved and ask them what their fees would be.

DISCOUNT REAL ESTATE BROKERS

You can also consider a discount brokerage. Until the mid-1980s, only the seller employed an agent. It was his/her money, after all. When it became apparent that the buyer often got the short end of the deal, the dawn of the buyer's agent era emerged. Commissions then were split between buyers' and sellers' agents. This is now the norm.

The real estate market became so hot in the first years of the new millennium that businesses sprang up just to service homeowners who wanted to sell their homes themselves. These kinds of brokers provide access to the MLS, legal oversight and other services. Often they're started by former Realtors.

Buyers who forego a buyer's agent can save money by negotiating for a share of the commission savings from the seller's Realtor. If you do this, make sure you specify all the things you expect to get with the house, including appliances, ceiling fans, window treatments, air conditioners, chandeliers, fireplace screens, awnings, etc. Inspect the home before closing to make sure the owner hasn't taken anything on your list.

Another area where you may forego a buyer's agent is when you buy a brand-new home just put on the market by a builder.

ADVANTAGES OF USING A FULL-SERVICE REALTOR

Even most For Sale by Owner sellers appreciate a buyer brought in by an agent and don't balk at the 3 percent commission they have to pay to that agent. (Remember: normally buyer's and seller's agents split the 6 percent commission.) A buyer's agent represents only you and your interests. They cannot tell the seller anything you tell them.

A buyer's agent will:

• **Increase your options:** As only Realtors have access to the Multiple Listing Services, they will be the ones to quickly and easily find you the largest number of homes. You can drive around by yourself, writing down phone numbers, but you could miss a side street that has your future home sweet home on it.

• **Bring you opportunities:** Realtors stay up to date on the current listings. They also have their ear to the ground as new listings are about to arrive. In a hot market, you can't depend on the real estate section in the newspaper or the open house sign to go up if the house is really for you. By the time you show up, the seller may already be fielding three offers.

- **Save you time:** An agent can go over your financial situation with you, prequalify you and help you get preapproved. They can help you brainstorm about your priorities and bring the listings that most closely match your situation. They explain all forms, lead you through the home buying timeline and tell you where and when you have to sign. If you're a very busy person or if you don't feel like you have the emotional energy to go through all this by yourself, an agent will be a great asset.

- **Find tested real estate professionals:** Usually your Realtor can recommend names of mortgage lenders, escrow companies, home appraisers, home inspectors, termite professionals and others involved in the home buying process.

- **Provide information about both the community and the home:** Often a Realtor has the inside scoop on who lives on the street, whether they have block parties often and just where they are in their family stage. They can also give you information about the community or city comparison of different areas, tell you about the taxes, the schools, the hospitals, and the crime rate.

- **Easy access:** It's the agent who has to get on the phone and ask when the home will be available for showing. You don't have to be the one leaving messages, waiting for a response or calling to follow up.

- **Experience:** Good agents have been through hundreds of homes. They will help you determine how to compare the house you are looking at to similar homes and their prices.

- **Do the dirty work for you:** If you don't like confrontation, be sure to hook up with an agent. The agent will bring your offer to the seller or the seller's agent and negotiate the selling price, terms and contingencies. If you're dealing with a For Sale by Owner house, you might feel much more comfortable letting the agent face the seller and make the deal.

- **Give you more credibility:** A seller may take a buyer represented by an agent more seriously. Agents usually prequalify buyers and encourage them to get preapproval from a lender. Sellers know that if a potential buyer is worth the agent's time, he or she is most likely worth the seller's time as well.

- **Keep you from missing deadlines:** It's the agent's job to keep you apprised of when to sign and where, when to transfer your funds, when to show up for the home inspection and when to attend any other important house transfer matters.

- **Saving money:** If you are both selling your current house and buying a new house, your agent will not be shocked or insulted if you try to negotiate his or her commission for the selling of your house.

FINDING A TOP-NOTCH AGENT

Chances are you see several real estate agent advertisements every day. You've just tuned them out. Now that you're ready to call one, how do you figure out which one will serve you best? The questions in the next section will help you determine the best agent for you. You can find agents' names and contact information by:

- going to open houses—the agents are usually the best-dressed in the house
- asking friends and family
- asking your company's relocation service
- entering the search terms "Realtor" and then the neighborhood you're thinking of in a search engine such as Google.com or Yahoo.com
- calling the area's chamber of commerce for a recommendation
- contacting the National Association of Exclusive Buyer Agents
- contacting real estate offices in the area or filling out the contact forms on their national websites.

The National Association of Exclusive Buyer Agents

Calling themselves "home buying experts," members of the National Association of Exclusive Buyer Agents do not work with sellers, nor do they work with a listing agent that represents sellers. They hold that only when an agent has no involvement with sellers are the buyer's interests truly represented. An agent representing both may try to push the homes they or their colleagues have listed.

An exclusive buyer's agent may have more training in the specific legal and financial aspects of buying a home. The National Association of Exclusive Buyer Agents provides this certification. To be registered, one has to abide by the detailed standards of practice set by that organization.

While this could be true, most reputable agents put their clients' needs first by showing them homes that fit those needs. An agent's reputation hinges strictly on how he or she performs for clients. If the agent starts showing clients inappropriate homes, the clients become dissatisfied quickly. Agents usually work in tight neighborhoods where word travels fast. A disgruntled client does not make for future business, and an agent knows this.

When interviewing an exclusive buyer's agent, try to get them to explain to you why they can represent you better than a traditional agent. Ask why they became a buyer's agent. If they impress you with their answers, put them on your short list. Don't be overly impressed strictly with the title, however. They do not seem to offer much more than the traditional agent.

The Agent Phone Interview

If you take even two or three of the above steps to find an agent, you'll be swimming in leads in no time. Your next step is to interview a few of them by phone. The following list of questions is reprinted in the *Realtor Questionnaire* on page 151. Be sure to copy these pages and fill out one for each agent you interview.

- **What price range of homes is your specialty?**
  Good Answer: About the same price range of homes you can afford.

- **In which neighborhoods do you sell the most homes?**
  Good Answer: The neighborhoods that interest you.

- **How long have you been a Realtor?**
  Good Answer: At least three years.

- **How do you communicate with clients?**
  Good Answer: Any way you like to communicate. Email, text messaging and of course the old standby—the phone.

- **How often do you communicate with your clients?**
  Good Answer: As close to daily as possible.

- **Do you have any special designations?**
  Good Answer: Each designation indicates the Realtor has gone through specific training on those specific issues. You may look for an RSPS, which is a Resort and Second-Home Property specialist, if that's the type of real estate that interests you. A list of the special designations is included at the end of these questions.

- **How many homes did you sell last year?**
  Good Answer: The national average is twelve, but twenty-four would be a nice number.

- **Are you a full-time agent?**
  Good Answer: Yes, absolutely. The more experience the Realtor has in different situations, the better.

• **How many buyers are you working with currently? How do you decide who gets to see the new listings first?**
Good Answer: Most agents are actively working with four or five buyers and sellers at a time. An agent working with ten or more individuals may not have the time to address to your needs.

Important Realtor Terms:

ABR®: Accredited Buyer Representative. This signifies expertise in representing buyers in their home purchase.

CIPS: Certified International Property Specialist. This professional is focused on international clients, including immigrants, foreign investors and local buyers investing abroad.

E-PRO®: Internet professionals with the knowledge and skills to put the power of technology and the Internet behind your real estate transaction.

GRI: Graduate REALTOR® Institute. This person is knowledgeable in all aspects of residential real estate (over 90 hours of training beyond license requirement).

AHWD: At Home With Diversity

CRS: Certified Residential Specialist

ABRM: Accredited Buyer Representative Manager

GAA: General Accredited Appraiser

ALC: Accredited Land Consultant

PMN: Performance Management Network

CCIM: Certified Commercial Investment Member

RAA: Residential Accredited Appraiser

CPM: Certified Property Manager

RSPS: Resort & Second-Home Property Specialist

CRB: Certified Real Estate Brokerage Manager

CRE: Counselors of Real Estate

SIOR: Society of Industrial and Office REALTORS®

Signs of a Good Agent:

- Works full-time at real estate
- Specializes in homes in your price range
- Specializes in areas that interest you
- Has at least three years' experience in the business
- Sells at least twenty-four homes each year (although the nationwide average is twelve annually)
- Will work exclusively for you and not be a dual agent
- Is computer/Internet savvy
- Has additional training, perhaps in negotiation
- Knows mortgage lenders, home inspectors, termite companies and appraisers who will provide these services at reasonable rates

You could be working with this person for months. Make sure your values and personalities match. Also, make sure your Realtor has extensive experience in representing buyers for the type and price range of homes that interests you. This agent will know when you go for your tours whether or not you can get even closer to your dream home than what he or she is showing you. Interview well because you may not be able to toss the agent on a whim. The agent will ask you to sign an exclusivity agreement to ensure you'll only work with him or her for either sixty or ninety days.

PERFECTING THE AGENT/CLIENT RELATIONSHIP

Hopefully, you've made sure that your personalities agree and you've gotten some details on your agent's background. Even if you've crossed all your t's and dotted all your i's, there can still be trouble in this relationship. Here are some warning signs of an agent who is not up to par.

An agent who is hard to reach and possibly rude when you call. This agent either has too many clients or doesn't know enough about the business to work at a manageable level of stress. Good agents take the initiative to stay in touch with you almost daily, even if only to say, "Nothing new was listed today!"

An agent who rushes you from house to house. This is usually the sign of the new agent who needs to get back out onto the street to show more houses to more clients. This agent is a bit panicked about whether he or she can make it in the real estate industry.

An agent who shows you homes outside of your price range. This agent might suggest that you "stretch" a bit, or show you homes that differ drastically from your needs and feigns ignorance when you bring this divergence to his/her attention. The good agents want to match you to a house so that their reputation remains good.

An agent who brushes off your questions, answers them in a condescending way or gives you vague answers. This could be the sign of either an arrogant agent or one who is not very experienced and therefore defensive. Keep your radar on for how much your agent seems to know about what's required for each form and when each step in the transaction process occurs.

An agent who shows you homes before getting an idea of what your financial situation is. The agent needs to help you understand just which homes you can afford and which homes you cannot afford. A sign of a good agent is honesty. The agent isn't your new best friend. If you want a $500,000 home but can only pay $2,000 per month, you're not going to be able to get that home. The agent is sometimes the deliverer of hard truths. Appreciate his/her honesty.

REAL ESTATE TRANSACTION TRENDS

Realtors provide a great service, making the home buying process easier and less stressful. They also keep their clients out of legal trouble, a service potentially worth thousands if not tens of thousands of dollars. However, you should know the objective truth about the alternatives to using a real estate agent. Here are some relatively new services that could help buyers and sellers save big bucks on home sales:

Bidding Websites: Buyers and sellers can enter property information and ask brokers to bid for their business.

Fee-for-Service Sites: Buy only the services you want, such as assistance completing paperwork or a Multiple Listing Service listing.

For Sale by Owner Sites: Sellers working without an agent account for almost 20 percent of the nation's annual home sales. These kinds of sites offer do-it-yourself information and allow sellers to pay a la carte fees to receive For Sale signs, property listings on the MLS and phone services that accept messages from potential buyers. Buyers can find homes that are not listed on the MLS on these sites. Your dream home may not be represented by an agent after all.

Referral-and-Rebate Sites: Potential buyers connect with agents at these kinds of sites. If they buy, the broker pays the site for the referral. In turn, the site gives part of that rebate to the buyer. These services are increasing in popularity and will continue to do so, particularly in soft markets where sellers are trying to save as much money as possible.

Most Importantly …

With the seller paying the bill for the agent's work, there are many good reasons for letting a professional lead you through the hunt for a home. However, it's possible to get a good deal if you find a home that the owner is selling on his own. This is because the seller would save the Realtor's commission.

You can also get a discount from a seller's Realtor if you find the home yourself and contact the listing Realtor directly. Since the listing agent will not have to share the 6 percent commission with the buyer's agent, he/she may be willing to give you some of the commission that the Realtor would have paid to your Realtor, if you had one.

Enjoy the help that an agent can provide, but don't turn the power over to them. Let them keep you on track without dictating your real estate choices. Keep your priorities at the forefront.

REAL ESTATE AGENT COMPARISON WORKSHEET

Use this worksheet to collect the contact information for all the potential agents that you have interviewed, and to record what their references have said about them.

	Agent #1	Agent #2	Agent #3	Agent #4
Name of Company				
Contact's Name				
Company Address				
Phone Number				
Email Address				
Web Address				
Reference #1 Name Phone number				
Reference #2 Name Phone number				
Reference #3 Name Phone number				
Reference #4 Name Phone number				

Ask the following questions to each of the agents you're considering working with. Then compare their answers. This will help you choose the right agent for you and your family.

Quality	Agent #1	Agent #2	Agent #3
Name			
Contact information			
What is the price range of homes you typically represent?			
Which neighborhoods do you sell the most homes in?			
How long have you been a Realtor?			
Do you have any special designations?			
Have you had any specialized training?			
How do you communicate with your clients?			
How many homes did you sell last year?			
How many buyers have you represented in the last year?			
Are you a full-time agent?			
How many sellers are you working with currently?			
How do you decide which home to recommend to whom?			
How many buyers are you working with currently?			
How do you decide who gets to see the new listings first?			

NOTES

INSPECTING YOUR HOME

When you're touring homes, make sure to keep an eye out for what could be serious defects in the house. The small actions and observations discussed in this chapter won't shock your Realtor or hurt the home. Don't be shy. This is most likely the largest financial transaction of your life. You will be hiring a property inspector to look over these things, but not until *after* you've made your offer.

WHAT TO CHECK DURING THE HOME TOUR

Flush toilets. Turn on lights. Make sure the oven and all heating elements come on, and check to see if the refrigerator is working. Open all the windows and try all the locks. Check that the vents in the bathrooms run well.

These are the simple problems that are easy to find and easy to fix. In some cases, an outward defect could indicate a serious problem. Knowing these things ahead of time could put you in a better bargaining position when you do make the offer. You could say, "I toured the house and noticed a long horizontal crack on the outside north-facing wall."

The following is a list of serious defects that may stop you from making an offer at all:

- **Cracks:** Any crack that you can stick your finger into is considered large. Look over the property's foundation, interior and exterior walls, fireplace, chimney and anything concrete (sidewalk, garage, patio). Keep in mind that these will have to be inspected closely. A diagonal crack means trouble. Watch out for these along a wall, foundation, or window. It means there is a stress on the existing structure. These kinds of cracks could occur anywhere but tend to appear more frequently in the corners. The diagonal crack could be caused by any number of things and is worth having an expert investigate.

  A vertical crack could appear due to the material drying process. For instance, a material such as the wallpaper or wallpaper trim could be shrinking.

A horizontal crack usually has to do with twisting of materials, and it is very much like the vertical cracks in that it could be superficial. However, if you do find something on the horizontal plane that is separating, then it needs to be explained by an expert.

- **Bubbles:** These often occur on the outside of buildings where caulking is no longer adhering properly. Or they could appear next to an inside window. Moisture could be coming in or around the frame of a window, or near a staircase.

- **Water Stains:** Check ceilings, walls and floors for discolored spots that may indicate roof leaks, pipe leaks or flooding. Feel the basement walls for moisture or dampness. Have your nose primed to pick up moldy smells. If there's a sunken pump in the garage or basement, run the other way. The home has had serious problems with water.

- **Stickiness:** All windows and doors should be able to open and close without problem.

- **Air-tightness:** You shouldn't be able to see light coming in around doors or windows.

- **Signs of Insect Infestation:** Mud tubes around the outside edges of houses are a sure sign that termites live there. Look for decayed and rotten wood by patios, fencing, swing sets and foundations.

- **Dirt Reinforcement:** Check the hillsides surrounding the property for netting or retaining walls, particularly if you are in an area known for unstable soils.

- **Slopes:** Sections of a building naturally run in a particular direction such as: flat, up and down, or at a specific angle. If a section of the building is moving in a different direction from its natural direction, then something is happening.

- **Baseboards:** Baseboards are mounted flush with the floor's surface at installation. However, a gap could develop over time between the bottom of the baseboard and the floor surface. This might be caused by structural movement.

Remember, don't try to determine the cause for various problems you see in the house. Your job on the home tour is to identify potential areas for concern. Later on you can ask for an evaluation from experts in home inspecting, structural engineering and architecture.

THE ALL-IMPORTANT INSPECTION AND INSURANCE HURDLES

Your offer is accepted, escrow has opened, and you're picking out towels for the guest bathroom. Just when you thought you could relax, you become all too aware that two out of every five houses have major defects. That's 40 percent.

There are two types of defects: patent and latent. Most states now require that sellers and real estate agents make full disclosures to prospective buyers of all known mechanical, structural and legal problems associated with the house. You would think these laws would protect you, and they do … for "patent" defects.

Patent defects are those problems that are known and easy to see. You don't need a professional property inspector to find a big crack down your living room wall or a patio cover hanging precariously by one bolt. The property inspector will be able to tell you whether these defects indicate greater damage (read: more money) or blemishes that can be taken care of inexpensively.

Latent defects, on the other hand, may remain hidden from even the most honest homeowner. They include faulty wiring, plumbing weaknesses, cracks in the foundation and other problems that lurk behind walls or in attics and basements. The property inspector can hunt these down.

WARNING! A brand-new home needs a home inspection just as much as the dilapidated fixer-upper. Contractors are notorious for rushing jobs and hiring inexperienced workers. All of the systems must be checked for defects. You'd be surprised how often windows are installed upside down, wiring is off and different tasks are left undone. Don't let the builder try to convince you that an inspection isn't necessary or that they have inspected it thoroughly themselves.

THE BEST INSPECTOR

Can you believe that most states don't certify, license or regulate home inspectors? Often, it's contractors who pull up to the side of your house with their official-looking trucks. Oh, and guess what … they can make the repairs as well! A home inspector who recommends you spend a bunch of money for their repair services operates under a clear conflict of interest. On the other hand, for a long time, inspectors did not have specialized training. It's hard to say which is worse: an inspector who sees you as a walking cash register or one who doesn't know what he or she is doing.

Things are becoming more rigorous now, but your best bet is still to go through the American Society of Home Inspectors, a professional association of independent home inspectors. To qualify for membership, an inspector has to have done 250 property inspections and have passed two written tests. Most home inspectors serve an apprenticeship of 500 to 1,000 inspections before becoming members. ASHI also has standards of practice that members must follow. Members take ongoing classes to keep them updated on the continually changing building codes. To find members in your area, call 1-800-743-2744 or visit their website at www.ashi.com, where you can search for someone qualified in your area. Expect to pay $300 to $800 for a home inspection, depending on your area.

Your Realtor may know a good, qualified inspector. When you get some numbers from your Realtor, don't just stop there. Make sure to ask the individual whether he or she is affiliated with the ASHI. It's wise to get their member number as well.

Below is a table that covers what the home inspector will be looking at and why.

Items	Examining Structure/Function
Roofing, chimney, gutters, vents, flashing and overhangs	Plugs in the chimney, broken tiles, leaks, proper drainage and structural stability
Foundation	Structural soundness
Heating and/or air conditioning systems	Proper operation and any unsafe conditions
Plumbing	Proper sink and tub drainage, water pressure level, signs of leaks, proper operation and any unsafe conditions of the water heater
Electrical	Faulty wiring, circuit breaker functioning, safe wiring at outlets and throughout the house
Doors and windows	Stickiness, fit, jams, proper lock function
Ceilings, walls and floors	Cracks, moisture problems, unevenness
Insulation and ventilation	Adequate insulation and proper ventilation, working fans
Basement and attic	Moisture, signs of flooding, mold, cracks in the floor
Septic tanks, wells, and sewer lines	Bacteria, leaks
Yard	Proper drainage, soil stability, integrity of fences
Garage	Moisture, cracks in floor, proper ventilation
Paint and window frames	Wear, need for repainting, rot on window frames
Kitchen	Appliance functionality, counter wear

Common home defects include: mold, poor drainage around the home, inadequate ventilation, faulty wiring, roof problems, heating or air conditioning defects, plumbing problems, poor home maintenance, water leaks around windows and minor structural damage.

WARNING! Many homes have radon levels over their safety limits. Radon gas is the second leading cause of lung cancer in the United States. Make sure this test is included in your home inspection. You can also purchase a radon test kit from a home improvement store. If the level is higher than four, the air is unsafe. For more information on this topic, go to www.epa.gov/aw/radon.

If you want to be particularly safe, you can buy errors and omission (E&O) insurance from the home inspection company. This covers defects found only after the inspector has left. Reputable inspectors carry errors and omission insurance.

Make sure you get more than a verbal report and even more than a checklist report. The report should include a detailed description of your specific property's mechanical and structural condition. Getting a sample report ahead of time will help you understand just what the inspection encompasses. Don't settle for some boxes checked off and some comments scribbled at the bottom. Your report should be typed in narrative form with several paragraphs covering an introduction, the home's exterior, interior, framing, plumbing, water heater, laundry, electrical system, heating system, cooling system, fireplace, kitchen, bathrooms and roofing. The *Home Inspector Questionnaire* on page 161 includes questions that you should ask when interviewing various home inspectors.

TIPS FOR GETTING A COMPLETE PROPERTY INSPECTION

• Contracting for home repairs often involves thousands of dollars. It's smart to make sure most of that money is coming your way, since you called for the repairs. You don't want to be handing wads of cash over to contractors after the seller is long gone. At the same time, the thought of pushing the seller to make many expensive repairs could be aggravating and even distasteful.

• One way to dodge both unappealing scenarios is to ask the seller's agent to come along with you on the inspection. The agent can then go back to his/her client, point out the problem areas and relate the discussion that transpired.

• Another advantage of attending the inspection is that you'll learn where important items are located in the home, including the furnace, the water heater, the circuit breakers and the emergency shutoff valves for the home's gas, electric and water systems. You'll learn which circuit breaker controls which rooms. Take a notebook as you'll be learning tons about what the home needs to be properly maintained. If you do go along, don't bring the kids or a bunch of your friends. They will only distract you from this important mission.

- When you get the inspection report, read it carefully. If you think something has been left out, call the inspector. Inspectors don't think they're done after locking the home's door behind them. They expect phone calls to clarify information in the report. Ask your inspector what he or she thinks would be reasonable repairs to ask the seller to pay for and fix. It's considered in bad taste to nickel and dime the seller for each loose baseboard or missing lightbulb. In fact, normal wear and tear on a house should be inserted into your offering price, not the home inspection where you must focus on the more severe defects that could change the value of the house. If your offering price is made on the expectation that the house will be in move-in condition, you have the right to request that problems be fixed.

Sellers are usually expected to repair:
- Termite damage
- Garage door malfunction
- Kitchen appliance malfunction
- Cracked windows
- Ripped screens

Areas of concern that may prompt you to withdraw the offer include: foundation problems (cracked, buckling, uneven), plumbing issues, electrical problems and mold.

PEST INSPECTION

The home inspector may notice insect damage, but he won't be performing an in-depth pest-control inspection. This is carried out by a separate company and will cost the seller anywhere from $75 to $225. If your home is wood and/or stucco, it's particularly prone to pest infestation. Even brick homes, however, can house some persistent pests.

PROBLEMS THAT COULD LEAD TO RENEGOTIATION

If there are repairs that you consider significant, you may need to consider making a response to the inspection. Ask the seller to renegotiate the price. The two of you are so far along, the seller will probably at least consider it without getting huffy and threatening to withdraw. If you have to pay $3,000 to repair the patio slab so that the rain runs away from the house, you could ask the seller to lower the price by $3,000. You could also let the seller get the problem fixed before you continue with the purchase. If the problem is quite serious, you can withdraw the offer, but the court expects you to give the seller a chance to fix it first.

You can also negotiate in the closing for the seller to make a list of repairs (like replacing the termite-infested garage door) before you move in. A cash settlement in lieu of fixing all repairs can make the deal sweeter for you, particularly if you are handy around the house. It can be more convenient for you to handle and arrange repairs if the seller is no longer occupying the home.

During the escrow process and even before, you are within your rights to have contractors come in and look at the problem and give you a bid. This can also convince the seller to see the price you're offering as reasonable.

If you want to check out what kind of repairs the home has undergone, you are within your rights to ask the seller to provide copies of prior insurance claims. You'll learn as much from the seller's reaction to this request as you do from the claim write-up itself. A reluctant seller could have something to hide.

HOME INSPECTOR CONTACT INFORMATION WORKSHEET

Use this worksheet to compare home inspectors available in your area and to make note on what their references have said about them. This will help you choose the home inspector that's right for you.

	Company #1	Company #2	Company #3
Name of Company			
Contact's Name			
Company Address			
Phone Number			
Email Address			
Web Address			
Reference #1 Name Phone number			
Reference #2 Name Phone number			
Reference #3 Name Phone number			
Reference #4 Name Phone number			

Ask the following questions to each of the inspectors you're considering working with. Then compare their answers. This will help you choose the right inspector for you and your family.

Question	Inspector #1	Inspector #2	Inspector #3
Name			
Contact information			
What is the price range of homes you typically represent?			
Are you a full-time property inspector?			
How long have you been in the business?			
How many homes would you estimate you've inspected?			
What certification do you have?			
Are you a member of the American Society of Home Inspectors or the National Association of Home Inspectors?			
How much will the inspection cost?			
Do you work in this neighborhood often?			
Are you familiar with the typical aspects of the home I need you to inspect?			
Have you inspected homes of the same materials, age and design?			
Do you offer errors and omission insurance (E&O)?			
May I look at a sample report?			
May I or my Realtor come along during the home inspection?			

NOTES

DISCLOSURE

Years ago when you bought a house, you often didn't know what problems might lurk within it. Over the past decade things have changed ... mostly due to litigations where buyers have sued sellers because of undisclosed defects. Now more than half the states in the nation require a disclosure statement from the seller as part of the standard real estate transaction. The disclosure statement describes the known problems within the property. However, it does not replace a home inspection report.

ITEMS TO WATCH IN A DISCLOSURE STATEMENT

What's not stated? The seller should state something definitive about the structure and function of features within the home. These statements include things like: no leaks in the plumbing, no cracks in the foundation. Look for what statements are omitted. It could be there's a reason for the omission that's far more significant than mere oversight.

Minimized details. A problem may appear to sound trivial but is far from it. Statements like "the lights sometimes flicker," or "there's a little spot on the ceiling" could be a cause for concern. Find out what the statements mean. Is there a faulty electrical system and a plumbing problem? Problems like these could be costly to fix.

HOW TO REJECT THE PROPERTY BECAUSE OF DISCLOSURE

Many states require an opportunity to reject a property based on disclosures. In California, a state with some of the toughest disclosure laws in the country, buyers have three days to back out of a property without risking penalty or loss of their deposit.

If your state doesn't have such a requirement, you can write it into the purchase agreement, which allows you to rescind the purchase without penalty. Make sure the clause you add includes a couple of days to review the disclosure statement, approve it or back out of the deal. Items in the disclosure statement can be used as a tool to renegotiate with the seller. You could agree to accept the deal as long as they fix the problem and/or lower the price.

SAMPLE DISCLOSURE FORM

The following is the format of the Transfer Disclosure Statement for the state of California (CAL. CIV. § 1102.4):

REAL ESTATE TRANSFER DISCLOSURE STATEMENT

This disclosure statement concerns the real property situated in the city of _____, county of _____, state of California, described as _____. This statement is a disclosure of the condition of the above described property in compliance with section 1102 of the civil code as of _____, 20____. It is not a warranty of any kind by the seller(s) or any agent(s) representing any principal(s) in this transaction, and is not a substitute for any inspections or warranties the principal(s) may wish to obtain.

I. COORDINATION WITH OTHER DISCLOSURE FORMS

This Real Estate Transfer Disclosure Statement is made pursuant to Section 1102 of the Civil Code. Other statutes require disclosures, depending upon the details of the particular real estate transaction (for example: special study zone and purchase-money liens on residential property).

Substituted Disclosures: The following disclosures have or will be made in connection with this real estate transfer, and are intended to satisfy the disclosure obligations on this form, where the subject matter is the same:

- Inspection reports completed pursuant to the contract of sale or receipt for deposit.
- Additional inspection reports or disclosures:

_____

_____

_____

II. SELLER'S INFORMATION

The Seller discloses the following information with the knowledge that even though this is not a warranty, prospective Buyers may rely on this information in deciding whether and on what terms to purchase the subject property. Seller hereby authorizes any agent(s) representing any principal(s) in this transaction to provide a copy of this statement to any person or entity in connection with any actual or anticipated sale of the property.

THE FOLLOWING ARE REPRESENTATIONS MADE BY THE SELLER(S) AND ARE NOT THE REPRESENTATIONS OF THE AGENT(S), IF ANY. THIS INFORMATION IS A DISCLOSURE AND IS NOT INTENDED TO BE PART OF ANY CONTRACT BETWEEN THE BUYER AND SELLER.

Seller _____ is _____ is not occupying the property.

A. The subject property has the items checked below (read across):

__Range	__Oven	__Microwave
__Dishwasher	__Trash Compactor	__Garbage Disposal
__Washer/Dryer Hookups		__Rain Gutters
__Burglar Alarms	__Smoke Detector(s)	__Fire Alarm
__TV Antenna	__Satellite Dish	__Intercom
__Central Heating	__Central AC	__Evaporative Cooler(s)
__Wall/Window AC	__Sprinklers	__Public Sewer System
__Septic Tank	__Sump Pump	__Water Softener
__Patio/Decking	__Built-in Barbecue	__Gazebo
__Sauna		
__Hot Tub __ Locking Safety Cover*	__Pool __ Child Resistant Barrier*	__Spa __ Locking Safety Cover*
__Security Gate(s)	__Automatic Garage Door Opener(s)*	__Number Remote Controls
Garage: __Attached	__Not Attached	__Carport
Pool/Spa Heater: __Gas	__Solar	__Electric
Water Heater: __Gas	__Water Heater Anchored, Braced, or Strapped*	__Private Utility or Other _____
Water Supply: __City	__Well	
Gas Supply: __Utility	__Bottled	

SAMPLE DISCLOSURE FORM

Sample Disclosure Form Continued

__Window Screens   __Window Security Bars   __Quick Release
                                                            Mechanism on
                                                            Bedroom Windows*

Exhaust Fan(s) in _____ 220 Volt Wiring in _____ Fireplace(s) in _____

Gas Starter _____ Roof(s): Type: _____ Age: _____ (approx).

Other: _____

Are there, to the best of your (Seller's) knowledge, any of the above that are not in operating condition? ___Yes ___No. If yes, then describe.

(Attach additional sheets if necessary): _____

_____

_____

_____

_____

B. Are you (Seller) aware of any significant defects/malfunctions in any of the following? ___ Yes ___ No. If yes, check appropriate space(s) below.

___Interior Walls ___Ceilings ___ Floors ___Exterior Walls ___Insulation ___Roof(s)

___Windows ___Doors ___Foundation ___Slab(s) ___Driveways ___Sidewalks ___Walls/

Fences ___ Electrical Systems ___ Plumbing/Sewers/Septics ___Other

Structural Components (Describe): _____

_____

_____

If any of the above is checked, explain. (Attach additional sheets if necessary):

_____

_____

_____

_____

* This garage door opener or child resistant pool barrier may not be in compliance with the safety standards relating to automatic reversing devices as set forth in Chapter 12.5 (commencing with Section 19890) of Part 3 of Division 13 of, or with the pool safety standards of Article 2.5 (commencing with Section 115920) of Chapter 5 of Part 10 of Division 104 of, the Health and Safety Code. The water heater may not be anchored, braced, or strapped in accordance with Section 19211 of the Health and Safety Code. Window security bars may not have quick-release mechanisms in compliance with the 1995 Edition of the California Building Standards Code.

C. Are you (Seller) aware of any of the following:

1. Substances, materials or products which may be an environmental hazard such as, but not limited to, asbestos, formaldehyde, radon gas, lead-based paint, fuel or chemical storage tanks, and contaminated soil or water on the subject property. __Yes __No

2. Features of the property shared in common with adjoining landowners, such as walls, fences, and driveways, whose use or responsibility for maintenance may have an effect on the subject property. __Yes __No

3. Any encroachments, easements or similar matters that may affect your interest in the subject property. __Yes __No

4. Room additions, structural modifications, or other alterations or repairs made without necessary permits. __Yes __No

5. Room additions, structural modifications, or other alterations or repairs not in compliance with building codes. __Yes __No

6. Fill (compacted or otherwise) on the property or any portion thereof. __Yes __No

7. Any settling from any cause, or slippage, sliding, or other soil problems. __Yes __No

8. Flooding, drainage or grading problems. __Yes __No

9. Major damage to the property or any of the structures from fire, earthquake, floods, or landslides. __Yes __No

10. Any zoning violations, nonconforming uses, violations of "setback" requirements. __Yes __No

11. Neighborhood noise problems or other nuisances. __Yes __No

12. CC&Rs or other deed restrictions or obligations. __Yes __No

Sample Disclosure Form Continued

13. Homeowners' Association which has any authority over the subject property.
__Yes __No

14. Any "common area" (facilities such as pools, tennis courts, walkways, or other areas co-owned in undivided interest with others). __Yes __No

15. Any notices of abatement or citations against the property. __Yes __No

16. Any lawsuits by or against the seller threatening to or affecting this real property, including any lawsuits alleging a defect or deficiency in this real property or "common areas" (facilities such as pools, tennis courts, walkways, or other areas co-owned in undivided interest with others). __Yes __No

If the answer to any of these is yes, explain. (Attach additional sheets if necessary.)
_____
_____
_____
_____
_____
_____
_____
_____
_____
_____
_____
_____
_____

Seller certifies that the information herein is true and correct to the best of the Seller's knowledge as of the date signed by the Seller.

Seller: _____   Date: _____

Seller: _____   Date: _____

PART 5:

NEGOTIATING LIKE THE PROS

NOTES

SECRETS OF WINNING NEGOTIATIONS

Satisfaction comes from knowing what you want in a house and understanding the sequence of steps involved in getting it. Once you've found your house, the atmosphere can be both exhilarating and nerve-racking. Knowing the ways real estate deals are typically transacted takes some of the uncertainty and stress out of the equation. When you know just what is up for grabs, then you can feel more confident about your purchase and pleased with everything.

First, keep in mind that home buying is fraught with emotion. If you lose a house, there will be another one that will suit you, perhaps even better. Don't risk making huge purchasing mistakes when you feel rushed—or forced to make a quick decision without enough information or time to think.

The first and foremost concern is your offering price versus the seller's asking price. After a little negotiating, the two of you will settle on a purchase price. Here are few things you should know about all three figures: the seller's asking price, your initial offering price and (after a bit of back and forth) the purchase price.

EVALUATING THE ASKING PRICE

Overpricing a home is a nationwide characteristic of sellers of all home sizes and income levels. Several reasons underlie the inflated value phenomenon. Buyers want a good deal. Sellers in turn, think buyers will be able to reduce their prices, so they set their prices higher than what the market would suggest. Usually sellers price their homes far higher than fair market value. Often because the agent wants the seller's business, he or she will present a marketing proposal that includes a high price. The agent hopes that dollar signs will flash in the owner's eyes, thereby prompting the owner to sign the agent's contract. Owners also tend to view an agent who prices the home high as competent and effective. The perception is that the agent has to be sharp since they recognized the home's great value, after all. Yet, when the home gets little or no interest, the agent suggests a price reduction. The home eventually sells below what the agent suggested initially.

Sometimes the seller won't listen to the agent who is trying to put a fair price on the home. The agent does work for the seller after all, so the agent has to list the home at whatever the seller insists. Overpriced homes may get some showings, but few or no offers. Your best bet in these scenarios is to walk away and wait for the price to drop.

The harsh reality of no one ringing the doorbell usually convinces the seller that their price is set too high. They may have the mindset that they put a lot of money into the house and are therefore entitled to recoup all of their costs. The market teaches them a lesson when other houses in the neighborhood sell more quickly than theirs. If a seller refuses your offer, the best strategy is to just walk away. Have your agent keep an eye on the property. Typically, that property's agent will keep in touch with your agent. When the price is cut, you'll most likely be the first to know. You can make another offer at that time. The seller will probably be more flexible the second time around.

Particularly if you are not working with an agent, a seller may try to convince you of why you should pay a higher price. The seller can base the price on several factors that have nothing to do with you. Here's what you should be on the lookout to disregard:

- The amount of money the seller needs to buy their next home
- How much is needed to pay off their loan
- What the seller spent on remodeling the home
- How much the seller paid for the home X years ago

None of these issues are relevant to you. All that matters is if the prices are comparable to homes sold. You are the one in the process of making the market.

THE ART OF MAKING THE OFFER

Agents depend on the prices of homes in the market and those recently sold to come up with a recommendation for an offering price. Good comparable market analyses or "comps" contain addresses, dates listed and sold, sale prices, number of bedrooms and bathrooms, parking, condition and remarks concerning houses similar to yours. The remarks section often includes the Realtor's reflections on the property. One important component of the comps is the price per square foot. This figure helps you compare homes more accurately. Usually, one or two of the homes stand out as having a much higher price per square foot than the others. These homes are usually overpriced.

If prices of the homes currently on the market are lower than those homes that have sold in the last six months, then housing prices are dropping and you're in luck.

Here is the basis on which both recently sold and currently listed homes are compared:

1. They are homes located in the same neighborhood.
2. They are the same age, size, condition.
3. They are prices from the past six months.

Make sure your comps include all houses on the market for both sets of comps (i.e. recently sold and currently listed). Keep in mind that the older the comp, the less it reflects fair market value.

Consider the economic environment. If a large manufacturer moved out of your area two months ago, the home prices from before that period do not reflect your current reality. Most likely, For Sale signs are cropping up faster than weeds. If you're in a rush because other offers are coming in, consider these factors as primary: lot size, number of bathrooms and flow of the floor plan. Refer to the *Making the Offer Worksheet* on page 182 when making an offer on a home or negotiating a deal.

GETTING AN APPRAISAL

It can be tough to weigh one house's amenities against another's and determine an accurate price. If buyers aren't lined up to make an offer on the home, you probably have the time to arrange to get a professional appraisal done. This is typically something the bank does during the escrow process. Getting it done before you even make an offer can reassure you of the fair market value of the home.

The appraiser will inspect the property, measure its square footage and examine the quality of construction. The amount of wear and tear, the functionality of the heating and plumbing systems and any damage to the house is also gauged by the appraiser. When a buyer orders an appraisal before the escrow process begins, he or she must pay the cost (several hundred dollars). Appraisals that occur after an offer is accepted, during the escrow process, are paid for by the seller.

If you're not that thrilled about parting with $300 to $800, here is where buyer's agents earn their money. Just because an appraiser prices house values all day long, it doesn't mean he or she knows the values better than the agent. On the whole, the Realtor will state a price very close to the appraiser's. Appraisers cover larger territories than your agent probably does. Unless you're really uncertain about the price your agent is suggesting, don't call an appraiser before the final sales contract is signed.

CONSIDERING YOUR MARKET

A Seller's Market

When many buyers compete for few homes, sellers can be picky. Not only do you have to come close to or exceed the seller's asking price, you have to be polite about it as well. The more contingencies you include in your offer, the higher your risk of losing the deal. Demanding repairs, new appliances or paint can prompt the seller to move on to the next offer. Your best option here is to look like the favored buyer in the pack. In other words, being preapproved and having a 20 percent down payment will help you stand out.

If you love and adore the house, but the seller doesn't feel the same about your offer, he or she typically has the power to bring you up in price. You won't have much bargaining power.

A Buyer's Market

In this market, you may think you can be as demanding as you want. And you could be, but the best results may not materialize. Given that there's so much emotion invested in a home, even if you are the only buyer, you could turn the seller off with ridiculous demands or super-low offers. The seller is within his or her rights to never field an offer from you again.

Don't get greedy and try to see how much you can get. Ask for what you'd like to have and what you (and your agent) think is reasonable. The seller can always say "no."

UNDERSTANDING HOUSING EMOTIONS

Moving is one of the top three highest stress inducers. Homes are filled with family memories, good and bad, and sellers are often ambivalent about the sale. A home is the equivalent of security, and sellers can experience overwhelming feelings of vulnerability at the prospect of giving it up. Whether they're trading up, trading down or renting, they are going out into an unknown. Besides putting feelings of nostalgia and security on a roller coaster, this negotiation involves the highest amount of money most people ever deal with in their lives. This could be financially sound or a foolish move. Lifestyles could be grievously affected from this point forward.

Finally, home buying and selling often occur as a result of significant life changes: birth, marriage, death or divorce. These changes alter one's identity. Is the seller becoming a retiree? A mother? A widower? There's a good chance the seller is in the process of trying to figure out who he or she is ... again. Along with these changes come stressful events that have nothing to do with selling their house. Nevertheless, they seep into that transaction and can bring trouble.

Changes bring stress. Sentimentality, financial risk and changing identity can all culminate in one thing: a potentially touchy, skittish, peevish seller. Do what you can to take the stress and upset away from the situation and you increase your odds of winning your price and contingencies.

Realtors can be experts at this. The Realtor acts as a buffer between you and the seller. Realtors have handled many touchy situations and have learned what works with different personality types. They know what to say and do when either of you becomes alarmed, upset or agitated. The least hysterical individual usually wins. If you have a difficult time keeping your emotions in check, you should certainly use a Realtor and hope the other side does as well.

WARNING! Beware of the agent who loses professional detachment. Everyone gets frustrated now and then, but if your agent snaps and can't get it back together, he or she won't negotiate very well for you either.

AVOIDING THE MOST STRESSFUL HOME BUYING SITUATIONS

During your home buying adventure, something will go wrong. The extent of that problem is largely up to you. You can minimize it or exacerbate it. Knowing what issues typically cause trouble before you encounter them will enable you to act quickly and with less stress.

Losing the House
Particularly in a seller's market, a seller may choose an offer other than yours. This outcome is a great disappointment for buyers, but it shouldn't send anyone into a panic. No matter how perfect the house seemed, there are other houses out there. Realtors remark upon how amazing it is when they hear a client discuss (sometimes bizarre) preferences and then find a home with just those things.

Going Over Your Time Limits
Most people think they should find what they need within thirty to sixty days. Going over these limits can make buyers feel hopeless. Rest assured that your house has just not come onto the market yet. At this time, you may start to panic and make bad decisions. If you're going for the home of your dreams, hold out for it. People have been known to search for a home for a year. If you're going to reside in one place for decades, pay the price up front in time and effort.

WHAT YOU CAN ASK THE SELLER

You have a lot more power than you think, particularly in a buyer's market. Here are a few areas you may not have considered when dealing with the seller. Get your Realtor's take on each option you'd like to negotiate. The Realtor should have hints about the seller's disposition—either from the seller's agent or, in a For Sale by Owner situation, the seller himself. Realtors know the negotiating "climate" and the market. The following suggestions cover some of the areas of the real estate transaction that can be negotiated.

- Ask the seller to pay some of the closing costs.

- Request that the seller pay for inspection, appraisal, title search, document fees, homeowner's warranty and so on.

- Say your offer is contingent on having your changes carried out. In a strong buyer's market, you can ask away!

- Ask the owner to make the offer "contingent upon the appraisal." If the appraisal comes back lower than the selling price, you might not even get your loan. Put a contingency in the contract stating that the seller will consider renegotiating the price if the appraisal comes in lower than your offer.

- Make the sale contingent upon selling your current home.

- Give the owner a short period of time to consider the offer. A period of 24 to 48 hours is long enough. (You can cancel your offer any time before it is accepted.)

- Ask for their furniture or their fixtures.

Personal Property to Consider
Too much time and money is wasted when home buyers and sellers go to court over fireplace screens and the like. Disputes about who owned the personal property at the time the deal was made are not uncommon. The rule strives to be simple and clean: property permanently attached to a building or land is technically a fixture and should be considered part of the home and therefore included in the purchase price. Some examples of fixtures include built-in appliances, screens, awnings, shutters and existing permanent light, including the chandelier.

The court uses these guidelines to determine a fixture:

Method of Attachment: nailed, bolted, glued, wired, built-in or cemented. While drapery rods are a fixture, the drapes hanging from them are not.

Adapted Items: an item that has been adapted to fit into the property. For instance, if blinds have been cut down to fit into the window, they will most likely be considered fixtures.

Buyer/Seller Intent: something listed in the contract clearly shows intent, so make sure you get everything into the contract that you orally agree to. If you want the refrigerator and the satellite dish, it's best to get it in writing. You might also consider listing items like curtains, microwaves, blinds and other appliances just in case.

In general, when the buyer and seller cannot come to an agreement and the case goes to trial, the courts tend to favor the buyer over the seller.

You may assume that some things that aren't tied down are part of the home. Bar stools that go with the kitchen counter could be there when you make you're offer, but gone on your move-in day. If the rug over the hardwood floor isn't glued down, it may be going with the seller.

Is That Fixture Included?
It's up to you to specify. Are these staying with the home or going with the seller? Homeowners can be surprised when they open the door of their new home to find it stripped. Look around the home for these items and never assume they're staying.

• Blinds	• Ceiling fans	• Chandeliers
• Curtains	• Dishwasher	• Dryer
• Microwave	• Oven	• Refrigerator
• Stove	• Washer	• Wall-mounted lighting

PROTECT YOURSELF WHEN MAKING YOUR OFFER

In an ideal world, a gentleman's agreement would do the trick. In the world we live in, however, it is important that you remember to write these stipulations in the contract. Specifically state:

• The amount of time you have to get financing	• The down payment amount
• The loan amount, not just a purchase price	• The type and term of the loan
• The maximum interest rate you will pay	

NEGOTIATING THE OFFER

Keeping in mind that home buying is an emotionally fraught undertaking, you can tailor your negotiation style to produce the best results. Let's say you find the dream home. Now give it some thought. Make sure you understand why you want the house (your motivation) and the value of the house (based on comps and appraisal). Make your offer that is slightly shy of your best price, particularly if you're in a seller's market. If you are in a buyer's market, however, you probably still have the time to make that lower offer, but come up quickly if the seller gets petulant about it. Sellers expect the offer/counteroffer process to go on for a while.

Let's say instead of the dream home you find an interim home. You can lowball (offer a price 25 percent to 30 percent less than the asking price) on an interim or starter home and see what reaction you get.

WARNING! If you don't have an agent and you're talking only to the seller's agent, know that he or she will let the seller know everything you divulge. For instance, if you tell the seller's agent you absolutely must have the house at all costs, that information will steel the seller against your lower bids.

It's important to first get an agreement on the price and terms of the sale. Worry about contingencies later. Two contingencies appear in nearly every offer: a financing contingency, which cancels the deal if the loan you've chosen in the contract isn't approved; and property inspection contingency, which allows you to cancel the agreement if you and the seller do not agree on the repairs.

Make your offer a price based on the facts you find in the comps. When the facts are right in front of them, sellers will be more motivated to deal.

After you submit your offer, sit back and take the time to decide what exactly you need to see in the seller's counteroffer to make the deal. Don't wait until you get it in your hands and have only 24 hours to respond. If the seller did not come close, don't give in. Remember, your points are important to you. Otherwise you wouldn't have stated them. You may be surprised to find the seller is bluffing. Give in on one or two things that aren't so crucial.

DEALING WITH THE COUNTEROFFER

It's a good sign when the seller responds with a counteroffer. The seller considered your offer and is willing to work with you. There will probably be a time limit in which you can respond. Make sure you understand everything the seller is saying yes or no to in the accepted offer. If you place a counteroffer, you or your agent can simply cross out the information on the counteroffer form and write in the new figures.

You may go back and forth many times before the deal is struck. Try to keep pride out of the negotiations. The seller is not trying to overpower you. Most likely, he's just trying to get a fair deal for a beloved home. Giving in on some points will probably end in an eventual win.

Sometimes if both buyer and seller are getting close to a final price but have stalled, the agent will suggest that you "split the difference." If you're offering $505,000 for a house and the seller states that he will go no lower than $525,000 consider coming up $10,000 to $515,000. The seller will have to come down $10,000. This also gives you the psychological satisfaction of thinking that you aren't outmaneuvered by someone more adept. When you split the difference, the final deal feels like a tie.

If you find you're going back and forth to a ludicrous extent, consider pulling out of negotiations. It will give you some time to reassess the house and your decision. It will also give the seller a wake-up call. After you've reassessed the situation and even looked at a few more homes, you are still free to make an offer on the home. By the time you do, the seller may have experienced a long, lonely week without a prospect in sight.

Once your offer is accepted or you accept a counteroffer from the seller, you go into the next stage of the escrow timeline.

WITHDRAWING AN OFFER

What if you make an offer on a house and the very next day (during the seller's short, 24-hour time frame to counter) an even more perfect house comes on the market? You won't be held liable for anything as long as:

1. The seller has not signed the offer. It's only when both parties sign the offer that it becomes a binding contract.

2. You're still in the offer/counteroffer process. In fact, in this case, you can just walk away from the last counteroffer, no reasons required.

3. One of the contingencies included in the offer are not met. If the home inspection reveals a cracked slab, you will probably be able to withdraw from the offer with no legal ramifications.

If none of these conditions apply to your case, but you just can't make this deal, the most you will probably lose is your deposit money. The seller may make noises about suing you for damages, but that usually costs more than it's worth. Most don't go through with it.

Sellers who back out of the contracts are liable for the expenses you've incurred from making moving preparations. Say you already paid the moving company $3,000 with the expectation that you'd be in that house at a certain point. A judge would most likely award you the $3,000, but you probably won't get the house.

TIPS AND SKILLS FOR NEGOTIATIONS

When stores have their sales, they mark down prices right on the item for all to see. No haggling occurs at the cash register. Because we're less familiar with the practice of negotiating for merchandise than those in other countries, Americans can feel uncomfortable about negotiating a price. It makes us feel impolite and even obnoxious. Haggling is the call of the day when dealing with home prices.

This process can be particularly tough when you run across a sharp negotiator who knows how to keep as much of his money as possible. These folks enjoy the challenge of a negotiation. Winning is a great success and worth all the stress of sometimes rancorous negotiations. Both sides have much to gain from making a successful real estate transaction.

If you are dealing with someone who is combative, be ready to walk away from the deal. They see concessions as defeats and enjoy winning every one of their points, no matter how trivial. You can try to manipulate them by setting up some contingencies that you don't really want and then letting them win on these. If you make it seem like not getting the new garage door or paying all closing costs is a big loss for you, this type of seller feels more powerful and may give in on the other contingencies that you really want.

These kinds of negotiators often make life hard for themselves and those around them. It's only natural if you feel exhausted from the whole process. Remember that you can walk away. There are other houses out there that you might like even more, and they won't come with a bulldog of a negotiator.

SELLER'S MARKET: THE MULTIPLE BID SCENARIO

In a hot market, buyers often place offers well above the list price. That's what happened when real estate sizzled in San Diego, Los Angeles, New York City, Boston and Washington, D.C., at the turn of the millennium. Homes sold in one day after receiving multiple offers. People who bid $10,000 to $20,000 higher than the asking price were stunned to find out that their competitor got it at $30,000 over list. Things have cooled considerably now, as builders have constructed more homes and real estate has appreciated. One never knows when—or where—that kind of market will boil up again. If it does, however, here are a few pointers for making yourself the seller's best prospect:

- Be preapproved.
- If you have stocks, consider selling them to boost your down payment to 25-30 percent or more. This will reassure the seller that your loan will be approved by the lender.
- Be generous. If the sellers need to stay in their home longer than anticipated, let them know that you're flexible on their move-out date.
- Require no repairs.
- Have a good offer on your current house. Reassure the seller that the transaction is going along fine.

Don't feel too humiliated after you have to practically sign over all your assets just to get a house. Yes, the seller holds all the cards in a seller's market. If the market is that hot, however, there is probably still some upside to go. In fact, it's likely that, if you get the house, it will appreciate quickly in the first year or two. The seller may be getting everything they want, but you are probably getting into a good investment. Don't feel slighted.

On the other hand, offering and counteroffering can be a frustrating process. Keeping track of your limits ahead of time will help you make the best decisions. Sometimes, irrationality can get in the way of a great deal if the seller insists his or her home is worth a price far higher than comparable homes. If the price turns you off, it's likely it's turning every one else off, too. Being patient and waiting for the price to come down can be your best strategy.

MAKING THE OFFER WORKSHEET

Make copies of this sheet so that you can keep a record of the details pertaining to any offers you make.

OFFER QUESTIONNAIRE

Address of the property:

Listing price:

Number of days on the market:

Market value:

Other offers rejected:

Are other buyers interested in the property?

Any related properties for sale?

What kind of market is this? Buyer's or seller's?

Can your agent anticipate multiple offers?

What is the condition of the property?

Does it need repairs?

Can you negotiate with seller for repairs?

Does the seller want to move quickly?

Has the seller already purchased another home?

Is the list price affordable?

Is the seller willing to pay closing costs?

Will the seller entertain seller financing?

What features and property are included in the sale?

Additional comments:

NEGOTIATING THE DEAL

Your offer price:

Number of days you want to be in escrow:

Closing date:

Seller's response to your offer (accepted/not accepted):

Reasons:

Counteroffer price:

Your response to the seller's counteroffer (accepted/not accepted):

Reasons:

New counteroffer price:

Seller's response to your counteroffer (accepted/not accepted):

Reasons:

PART 6:

MAKING THE PURCHASE

NOTES

CLOSING TIME – GETTING THROUGH ESCROW

The escrow process can feel like a desperate race, but by being organized and knowledgeable, you will coast through it. There certainly are numerous steps in the escrow process, but the escrow officer and your real estate agent will lead you through them.

THE ROLE OF THE ESCROW OFFICER

Sellers want a deposit so that they are sure you're a serious buyer, but you certainly aren't about to write out a check to them. What if they are scam artists? What if they don't agree to your terms? The real estate brokerage doesn't have the capacity to handle the transfer of funds. The mortgage lender is on your side and deals only with providing you with funds.

With every other entity on someone's side (for all intents and purposes), a neutral third party is required. That party is the escrow officer. This person makes sure everything is on the up and up on both the buyer's and the seller's part. Once you have a signed contract, then copies of the documents and your checks for the deposit and eventually for the whole amount of the loan are turned over to the escrow officer.

Escrow fees can be anywhere from a few hundred to a few thousand dollars. You can search the Internet to get an idea of local escrow costs. There are many fees involved in escrow. Who pays what depends on the area in which you live. Sometimes the buyer pays; sometimes the seller pays; and in some places the costs are split in half. In some parts of the country, the real estate agent controls his or her own escrow account.

WARNING! While an escrow officer usually acts as a neutral party to the transaction, it is possible that he or she works exclusively for your lender. In that case, fees could be higher. After getting a rundown of the office's fees, ask the officer who he represents. If the answer is your lender, you might want to shop your business around town a bit before settling with this escrow office.

Escrow is charged with being a neutral third party. They take that duty seriously. Sometimes they even come across as the automatons of the real estate process. They don't get excited either for you or for the seller. The escrow office acts as a safe custodian for funds and documents; a clearinghouse for all fund transfers and a clerical service to transact the details of the settlement of accounts. During the escrow period, titles are transferred, financing is finalized, any liens are discharged, inspections are performed, and disclosure papers are signed. Closing procedures vary from state to state.

ESCROW CHECKLIST

You've reached an agreement with the seller. Both of you have signed the purchase contract. That means you have a "ratified offer." You're ready to start the escrow process. Now, you're going to need to take five important steps:

1. Gather your documents.

Financing: You will need the cashier's check for the full purchase amount or the commitment letter from your lender that shows you have the money to buy the home. Bank statements proving you have the down payment in cash are also needed.

Homeowner's Insurance Policy: The lender doesn't want to take any chances that its investment (the house) will not be protected, even for a day. The lender will not approve the loan without a homeowner's insurance policy. Start working now to find the best, most reasonable homeowner's insurance policy.

Special Insurance: If the home is situated on a flood plain, in tornado alley or amid an earthquake prone area, you may require special insurance. Again, the lender needs proof of this insurance before closing the loan.

2. Complete any repairs that you have agreed upon with the seller or that the lender requires.

FHA, VA or other types of government-backed loans may insist on having certain things repaired before closing escrow. If your agreement specifies the seller will be making certain repairs, then you need to keep track of them through your agent. The agent can visit the house to make sure the process is going smoothly and according to your instructions.

3. Have the property inspected.

In most states, the buyer pays this cost. The sooner you get the inspection done, the better. That way, there will be plenty of time to address any glitches in the repair process.

4. Go on the final walk-through.

In most cases, the final walk-through is just a formality to ensure that the property has not been damaged in any way since you first made the offer on it. It's also a good idea to check that the electrical, plumbing, heating and cooling systems are still working well. If there have been changes or something is not working, the contract is in question and negotiations need to be opened again. Most Realtors put the final walk-through requirement in the contract. Just make sure to do your walk-through a few days before close of escrow. You might need the extra time to resolve any issues you want to bring up. Remember to check the personal property in the home. Are the appliances and fixtures that the seller agreed to leave still there? Did the sellers leave anything for you to haul away not agreed upon initially? If so, you need to be reimbursed for your time and expense. Here's a list of things you should pay special attention to on the final walk-through:

- What is the condition of the property?
- Does it look the same as when you first visited?
- Has it fared for the better or worse?
- Did the seller do all the agreed repairs?
- If not, what arrangements are in the works?
- Has the seller forwarded their mail?
- Have all utility companies been notified that the seller is moving?
- Did the seller transfer the utility services to your name?
- Is there still personal property on the premises?
- What, if any, are the arrangements for it?
- Did the seller show you where manuals are for the stove, washer dryer, etc.?
- Do you know where the seller will leave the keys and garage door opener?
- Do you know the maintenance schedule for items in and outside of the house?

5. Go to closing and remember to bring these items:

- Your driver's license or photo identification
- Homeowner's insurance policy and its receipt for prepayment
- Loan commitment letter from your lender (or a cashier's check for the full amount)
- Cashier's check for the down payment and payment of closing costs
- Personal checks in case there are unexpected charges
- Lender's initial statement of settlement charges

Closing To Do List	Due Date	Completed
Go over closing costs estimates.		
Find out how to hold title.		
Get title insurance.		
Get homeowner's insurance.		
Arrange for down payment and closing costs to be ready for escrow closing.		
Get the loan documents ready.		
Make sure the seller completes all the repairs agreed upon prior to closing.		
Do a final walk-through inspection.		
Go over closing documents.		
Make sure seller hands over keys and garage door opener.		
Sign all closing documents.		

DOCUMENTS YOU WILL RECEIVE DURING ESCROW CLOSING

1. **"Truth in Lending" statement.** This tells you the true interest rate on your loan, as well as the terms of the loan, finance charge, amount financed and the total payments required. Look over these figures carefully.

2. **The mortgage or deed of trust.** This is the lien the lender holds against your home. If you default on your mortgage, the lender owns the property. Despite the fact that the bank has put up the majority of the money, in the eyes of the law at least, you own the home. You are responsible for the property, and its benefits come only to you.

3. **The deed.** This indicates that you are now the owner of the property. Consider putting this document in a safe deposit box at your bank or in a safe in your home.

4. **The final closing statement.** The deed isn't the only crucial paper you'll be taking home. The final closing statement lists all the money related to your home purchase that went into escrow. Keep a copy of this for your income tax return. Loan origination fees and property tax payments are tax deductible. When you get the closing statement, file it in a safe place.

DOCUMENTS YOU WILL SIGN DURING CLOSING

Typically, the closing is an official meeting attended by the buyer, the seller and their real estate agents, as well as a representative from the lending company. One of the most time-consuming and intimidating aspects of the closing is that you will have to sign page after page of documents. Here are a few of the forms you will be asked to review and sign.

1. An affidavit that you'll use the property according to zoning laws.

2. IRS forms for the sale or purchase of the home.

2. A compliance agreement, wherein you agree to re-sign documents if there are any mistakes made by any parties.

3. A sanity document, which attests that you have not been declared mentally incompetent, are employed, are over 18 and meet a few other personal requirements.

ESCROW COSTS

There are two kinds of escrow costs. Closing costs are due when escrow closes. The other escrow cost does not relate directly to the closing of escrow and is called "POC" or paid outside of closing.

Title Charges:

	Date Paid	Amount	Notes
Settlement fee	Close of escrow	$150 - $400	A separate company does the title settlement.
Title search and insurance	Close of escrow	$200 - $500	Depending on where you live, either the buyer or the seller pays this fee.

Government Recording and Transfer Charges:

	Date Paid	Amount	Notes
Recording fees	Close of escrow	$25 - $100	
Transfer charges	Close of escrow	$10 - $100	The county, city or state wants a little of the money flying around.

Loan Costs:

	Date Paid	Amount	Notes
Points	Close of escrow	0-2 percent of your loan amount	Tax deductible. Buyer pays advance.
Loan origination fee	Close of escrow	About 1 percent of the loan amount	The rules fluctuate, but this is probably not tax deductible. Consult a tax advisor to be sure.
Assumption fee	Close of escrow	Varies	This only applies if you are taking over the previous owner's mortgage.
Application fee	When you first apply for the loan	$50 - $350	Ask the lender if it can be waived.
Appraisal fee	When you first apply for the loan	$100-$500	Sometimes this is included as part of the application fee.
Home inspection	During escrow at time of inspection	$300 - $1,000 for home inspection $100- $500 for pest inspection	
Processing fees	Close of escrow	$100-$900	Mail or delivery fee for overnight shipping.

Taxes:

	Date Paid	Amount	Notes
Property tax prorations	Close of escrow	Thousands of dollars	If you move in three months after the seller has paid six months worth of taxes, you may have to settle with the seller.

Miscellaneous:

	Date Paid	Amount	Notes
Survey	Close of escrow	$400 - $1200 or more	The lender may need a surveyor to make sure there are no encroachments on your property.
Condo and co-op fees	Close of escrow		There may be a move-in or association transfer fees.

TIPS FOR AN EASY, LOW-COST ESCROW

Reduce prepaid loan interest. You can time your first loan payment well if you play your cards right. Never schedule your escrow close on a Monday. The lender has to put your mortgage funds into escrow the preceding Friday. Then you are charged interest on your loan for Friday, Saturday and Sunday, even though you won't own the home until escrow closes on Monday. It's better to close escrow on any other weekday.

Meet with your escrow officer. Under the avalanche of so much paperwork and the cacophony of phone calls, steps can go astray during your escrow. Documents get lost. Important facts are miscommunicated. When something goes wrong, you want someone who cares at least a little to work on rectifying it. To get that compassion, you want the officer to be able to connect a name with a face. It's not a bad idea to go into the escrow office and meet your escrow officer. Call the officer and give him or her all your phone numbers and where you can be reached most easily. Ask if you need to provide any more documents or information.

Stay in touch with your lender and your escrow officer. These folks have many clients. Your files could get buried under stacks of other paperwork. To keep your files at the top of the pile, check with each of these people once a week to make sure things are going smoothly. With all the home buyers they're keeping tabs on, they'll probably appreciate that you initiated the phone call. Most likely, they'll use the opportunity to mention that they needed one document or another. This facilitation that you provide will speed up the whole process.

Keep the lender, escrow officer and real estate agent aware of your whereabouts. If you are going to leave town, make sure everyone knows where to reach you. You can always fax or overnight a document from a remote location as needed. If you miss a signing deadline, you could lose the loan, the house or that low interest rate you were so lucky to get.

Resist the temptation to fix up that vacant home before escrow closes. If your new home is vacant, it may seem like good common sense to want to get right into the house and start fixing it up or cleaning it even before escrow closes. It's sitting there just waiting for your magic touches! This is not a good idea. If the loan doesn't go through or something happens with the seller's title to cancel the sale, you could have spent time, effort and money fixing up someone else's house. You cannot recoup those costs. Further, if the house catches fire or is flooded during that time, you don't have insurance to cover the expense for repairs. It's better to allow some time to do these tasks after escrow closes.

TAKING TITLE IN THE PROPERTY

How you define title or ownership in the property is important, particularly if you are buying with a spouse or even a business partner. The most important stipulation involved in title is the consequences upon the death of one of the parties. Do you want your share of the home to automatically go to the other owner in the event of your death? Or, do you want to name a beneficiary for your share? The various ways to take ownership of your house are as follows:

Sole Ownership: Clearly, this is for the single person. You are the only owner. You have no cosigners. Even if your loan does have a cosigner, the home may have only your name on the deed.

Joint Tenancy: This is the most common form of ownership. Two or more people agree that any of the owners can sell their interest to whomever they want without permission from other owners. Upon the death of one owner, the survivor gets the deceased's share. If you're in a long-term, committed relationship or are married, you might select this title.

Tenancy in Common: Unlike joint tenants, tenants in common choose beneficiaries to receive their share of the house if they pass away. It doesn't go automatically to another owner. This is the choice for those buying a home with a relative or friend.

Tenancy by the Entirety: This option is provided only to married couples. In this agreement, both parties must agree to sell or refinance the home. Upon the death of one spouse, the other gets the entire home without having to go through probate.

TROUBLESHOOTING YOUR ESCROW

The escrow period is a busy time for both buyer and seller. Escrow offices are typically frantic. Problems occur, if for no other reason than oversight. The home buying process is rife with potential misunderstandings and human error. It's good to go over this section in case problems occur. This way you'll know what steps to take, and you'll resist the urge to panic.

Money Disputes
There are so many financial figures flying around, you're bound to be surprised by one or two of them when you sit down to sign at escrow. The lender should have prepared an estimate in writing for a range of the closing costs when you applied for the loan. In case discrepancies arise, bring that document with you to the signing. If any of the costs are out of line with what you thought the estimated figures were, refer to the original estimated costs statement you filed away. Show it to the escrow officer. If someone has to make some calls to straighten out the situation, let them. It won't hurt to extend escrow a day or two.

Loan Problems
If anyone is a day late getting a signature or a cashier's check in to the escrow office, the documents may not be prepared by your closing date. Closing can always be extended for one or two

days. Remember that on some faxed documents the signature can be considered original. Don't forget about overnight mail.

Walk-through Wackiness

This can be a tricky area. It's probably best to let go of minor problems. For instance, if the owners have dinged the walls in moving their furniture, it's not going to cost much to go to a home improvement store for a quart of touch-up paint. If they've left a great deal of trash that will need to be hauled away, you may want to consider offering to make the arrangements, but they need to pay for it. Finally, if they have taken an item you specified or assumed would stay, try to straighten it out. Remain calm and deal with things rationally so they get done as quickly as possible.

Title Hold-ups

Unfortunately, these do occur, and they can take weeks to straighten out. Your title insurance can cover most of your expenses that result from changes in moving plans, hotel costs, etc.

Seller Cannot Move Out on the Agreed Upon Date

Home buying and selling depends on many parties, and often one party's plans get thwarted if another party's plans get delayed. If the seller's new housing situation doesn't pan out when expected, the seller may ask for a "rent-back." Often after a home purchase is transacted, the seller arranges with the buyer to rent the home back for a temporary period of time. The most common way to set the price is to add what you're paying monthly for principal and interest, property taxes and insurance. The total can be prorated on a per diem basis if the sellers are staying less than a month. A smart move is to ask the escrow officer to hold four weeks of PITI plus Private Mortgage Insurance (PMI) in escrow before it is transferred to the seller. This gives you a buffer in case something happens and the sellers still cannot move.

Most Importantly ...

Just remember that escrow is more annoying than confusing and overwhelming. If you use a real estate agent, he or she should direct you in what you need to get from whom and when. If you don't use an agent, you'll be poring over this book page by page. You can stay on top of the process and avoid a great deal of stress when you know what to expect in the escrow process.

Once all is said and done, you can celebrate a new home and a new life. Congratulations! You deserve a rest and a good pat on the back.

CLOSING COSTS WORKSHEET

Use this worksheet to determine all the costs in purchasing your home.

Loan Costs

Type of Cost	When Paid	Amount	Notes
Points			
Loan origination fee			
Assumption fee			
Application fee			
Appraisal fee			
Home inspection			
Processing fees			

Title Charges

Type of Cost	When Paid	Amount	Notes
Settlement fee			
Title search and insurance			

Government Recording and Transfer Charges

Type of Cost	When Paid	Amount	Notes
Recording fees			
Transfer charges			

Taxes

Type of cost	When Paid	Amount	Notes
Property tax prorations			

Miscellaneous

Type of Cost	When Paid	Amount	Notes
Survey			
Condo and co-op fees			

CHOOSING THE RIGHT INSURANCE COMPANY

Most homeowners have too little insurance. When the big floods and fires hit, the terms "underinsured" or "uninsured" reverberate all over the media. News accounts in these situations report on families wiped out, their whole assets lost. You don't want to be in this situation, particularly if you live in an area prone to fires, floods, hurricanes or earthquakes. A difference of a couple of hundred dollars a year could bring peace of mind and protection should disaster strike.

The lender is going to require that you purchase an insurance policy up front. Here are a few ways to save on your homeowner's insurance.

- Purchase a home security system. With their investment protected, the insurance company won't consider you as big a risk.

- Make it clear to the insurance company that no one in your home smokes. Smokers burn houses down by falling asleep with lighted cigarettes.

- After three years have passed, call to see if you can get a reduced premium for staying with the same company for so long. If they say no, ask when you might get a reduced premium. Some insurance companies reduce premiums by 10 percent if you're a customer for six years or more.

- Buy your car insurance from the same carrier.

- Let them know if you're about to retire. Retirees are home more, so they are more likely to catch problems around the house before they get out of control.

- Check with your employer, business or alumni association about whether they have a discounted homeowner's insurance program.

CHOOSING THE RIGHT INSURANCE COMPANY

There are six forms of homeowner's insurance. The lender is likely to have a minimum amount of coverage required. Be smart. This is the most valuable asset you own. Don't try to cut too many costs. Focus instead on what it would take to get the job done.

Those in the industry code the insurance policies from the least coverage to the most coverage by saying HO-1, HO-2, HO-3, HO-4, HO-5 and HO-6. Here is a handy reference guide for deciding what insurance you need.

Insurance	Policy	Coverage
HO-1	Basic Policy	Covers fire, windstorm, explosion, smoke, broken glass and other perils including theft, vandalism and liability.
HO-2	Broad Form	Covers the same as HO-1 but adds several items. For instance, this type of policy may protect against damage from burst pipes, exploding furnaces, collapse of the building and falling objects.
HO-3	All Risk Form	Covers everything not specifically excluded. May cover features that are part of the structure (for example, wall-to-wall carpeting). It bundles up all the extra type of riders that might be available with other policies such as included coverage for jewelry and furs. It can even include coverage for sewer backup and building code upgrades.
HO-4	Renter's Policy	Protects the renter's personal possessions. Covers everything in HO-3, plus some.
HO-5	Comprehensive	Exclusions are usually listed. This is the most expensive type of insurance.
HO-6	Condo or Co-op	Insurance used for condominiums and cooperatives.

When choosing insurance, you don't have to stick to the lender's minimum requirement. Determine the replacement cost of your home and personal property. Getting a square footage price from your local home builder's association is helpful. They may even have figures for your neighborhood. Consider how much your personal property is worth. To get the best results, use a pen and paper to write down all furniture, art, musical instruments, electronics, books, jewelry, clothing, kitchen supplies and cars you currently own. When you buy new things, it's wise to keep your receipts. If there is a flood or other natural disaster, you'll have proof of the value of your belongings.

The amount of coverage you need is only one stipulation. Make sure you get a policy with a "guaranteed replacement cost" provision. With this in place, the insurance company has to rebuild the home, even if the costs exceed the policy limits. If the insurance company underestimated your square footage, they are still liable for the actual costs.

You can save money with a higher deductible versus a lower one. Signing on for a $500 deductible rather than a $250 deductible reduces your premium by approximately 15 percent. Increase the deductible to $1,000, and you'll pay approximately 25 percent less than a policy with a $250 deductible.

Understand the terms of your policy and what is and isn't covered before you report damage. These questions help you gauge which policy will work the hardest for you.

- How often are rates increased?
- Will my insurance go up if I file a claim?
- How do you define guaranteed replacement coverage? (It could be only up to 110 percent of your policy's total dwelling coverage. If replacement costs 125 percent, you're going to be paying significant out-of-pocket costs.)

OTHER ASPECTS OF HOMEOWNER'S INSURANCE

Lawsuit Protection

If someone on your property has an accident, you could be responsible for medical bills and other damages. Even the best of friends have to have their medical bills paid. If you are clearly negligent, you would probably want to cover any medical expenses anyway. If this sounds like a good plan to you, carry enough liability insurance to protect at least two times the value of your assets. In fact, if you have assets totaling more than $300,000, you might consider what's called an "umbrella" or "excess liability" policy.

Personal Property Protection

Personal property coverage usually runs about 50 percent to 75 percent of dwelling coverage. (Keep in mind that dwelling coverage does not include the land.) For this aspect of the insurance policy, make sure that you get "personal property replacement guarantees" that pay you for the replacement cost of an item rather than its amortized value. If your insurance agent tells you that this is not standard procedure, ask for it to be put on as a "rider" or an addition.

If the item is lost, stolen or damaged, how will you prove its value to the insurance company? A smart thing to do is to videotape your belongings and document any appraisals you've gotten for different pieces. Be sure to store this documentation somewhere outside of your home.

After you've decided what features you want in your home insurance policy, you can search the Internet or call an insurance broker to find the lowest cost and the most reputable firm.

Catastrophe UN-Coverage

In many parts of the United States, natural disasters are not covered by your insurance policy. For instance, because of earthquake risks, no typical insurance company will insure homeowners in the most dangerous areas of San Francisco. Some suburbs of the same city offer it without hesitation. Make sure you know just what is and is not covered in your policy. Ask the insurance company what is covered beyond the most common eleven perils? (The most common eleven perils are fire or lightning, windstorm or hail, explosions, riot or civil commotion, damage caused by aircraft, damage caused by vehicles, sudden or accidental damage from smoke, vandalism or malicious mischief, theft, volcanic eruption, damage by glass or safety-glazing material that is part of a building.) See the *Insurance Agent Comparison Worksheet* on page 200 for more questions to ask.

Flood Insurance: If you are in a community at risk for flooding, the standard insurance policy probably won't cover your home. You have to ask expressly for a "rider" or an additional part to the policy.

Earthquakes: Active fault lines run throughout much of California and even parts of the Midwest. In some areas, the states carry earthquake insurance. Check with your insurance company to find out just what would happen if your home were damaged in an earthquake.

TITLE INSURANCE: PROTECTING YOUR INVESTMENT

The bank protects its interest by insisting on title insurance. This form of insurance is a guarantee that the title or ownership deed to the house is yours free and clear. The title insurance fees go to researching who legally owns the property. If there could be tax liens on it or judgments against it, the seller does not own the property outright. You only have to pay these fees once (unless you want to refinance your mortgage).

There are two kinds of title insurance. Most people get a "standard title-insurance policy," which is less expensive than the extended title-insurance policy. Standard policies cover the usual problems: fraud, defective recordings, tax assessments, judgments and property defects found after a search of public records. The "extended title-insurance policy" covers all of the above, plus things like a faulty land survey or a change in zoning laws. Extended title insurance covers the trickier problems that aren't usually the result of outright fraud.

Remember, the home inspector's task is to discover all potential flaws in the home. If all goes well, it should put your mind at ease that you're investing in a substantial home. Likewise, you need to put a price on peace of mind when selecting insurance. While an HO-5 policy may cost 15 percent more than an HO-3 policy, the additional coverage may be worth it to you.

INSURANCE AGENT CONTACT INFORMATION WORKSHEET

Because there are so many types of coverage, you should explore all your options before picking a homeowner's insurance policy. This worksheet lets you keep track of your top four picks.

	Company #1	Company #2	Company #3	Company #4
Name of Company				
Contact's Name				
Company Address				
Phone Number				
Email Address				
Web Address				
Reference #1 Name Phone number				
Reference #2 Name Phone number				
Reference #3 Name Phone number				
Reference #4 Name Phone number				

INSURANCE AGENT COMPARISON WORKSHEET

This worksheet gives you some important questions that you should ask in order to choose an insurance agent who is right for you.

	Company #1	Company #2	Company #3
Name of Company			
Contact's Name			
What is the price range of homes you typically represent?			
What is covered beyond the most common eleven perils?			
What is not covered?			
Can I raise my coverage later?			
Will I get amortized costs or replacement costs of my home and possessions?			
What is the deductible?			
What is the liability limit?			
Do you offer any discounts if I also have my auto policy with you?			
What is the typical turnaround time for a claim?			
When filing a claim, do I obtain and submit my own estimates, or does an adjuster visit my home?			
How many claims can I file before I am dropped from the insurance policy?			

PART 7:

MOVING

NOTES

MOVING TO THE NEW HOME

Make the moving process easy by using *The Pre-Move To-Do Checklist*, the *Address Change and Record Forwarding Worksheet* and the *Service Cancellation Worksheet* provided in this book. These documents do the thinking for you, so that you don't have to remember every vendor and service that has your old contact information in their database.

Some people move the day the escrow closes, but that can be tricky if the seller is moving out the same day. It's considered better to wait until the seller has been out a day. Moving day is stressful for everyone. Why make it more so by carrying in your stuff while the seller is still moving out?

A better idea is to let the house stay empty for a few days to a week while you paint, clean and get acquainted with it. It's so much easier getting things done with no boxes to trip over. The unpacking process will be difficult enough.

LOCAL OR NATIONWIDE MOVERS

Your choice is usually between local movers or the large nationwide companies. Because there are so many to choose from (and many are often shady), your local Better Business Bureau's listing of movers will be a good place to start. When it comes to moving your precious possessions, it's better to pay a little more for quality, particularly if you are moving across the country.

How is the cost of a move calculated? Intrastate moves of under 40 miles are estimated on an hourly rate or based on cubic footage of the goods. Interstate (between states) moves are based on distance and the weight of the goods.

Moving companies are busiest from April through October and during the summer months. Because it's so busy in July, August and September, it's a good idea to get all contracts in writing. Moving companies do double book to make up for the slow winter months. When you sign the moving company's contracts, make sure the date and time for their arrival is in writing.

Moving companies assume different levels of liability for the value of what they transport. Make sure you know just how much is covered. If you are moving high-priced collectibles, let the moving company know, and you can talk together about getting extra insurance. Your homeowner's insurance may even cover your move.

Questions to ask the movers:

- Are you available on the date that I need to move?
- Are boxes included in the estimate?
- Is the cost for packing included?
- If not, what is the fee for this?
- How many movers do you include?
- What is the cost for getting an additional mover to help?
- What is the cost for insurance to move?
- Is additional coverage available?
- Can you explain your policy for damaged boxes?
- Do you take credit cards? If so, which ones?
- Can you give me at least three trade references?
- Are you a member of the Better Business Bureau?
- What is your cancellation policy?
- What is your payment policy?
- Do you have liability insurance?

MOVING TIPS

Get organized. For the few weeks before your move, leave the cars outside and cordon off the garage so you can start packing and organizing your boxes. You can use masking tape across the floor or just think of general areas where you will set up the sections for your boxes, such as: garage sale, Goodwill, garage, storage, living room, dining room, kitchen, master bedroom.

Set aside items you'll need right away in your new home. Make sure you take the following items in a suitcase you'll keep close to you: bed linens and pillows, towels and washcloths, toiletries, medications, nightwear, work clothes, extension cords, shelf liners, lamps, garbage bags, paper plates, plastic wrap, paper towels, soap and sponges, pet bowls and food.

Label each box. Write the name of the room where each box will be going. That way, the movers will know where to put items without asking you on moving day.

Keep the children preoccupied. Families with young ones should consider having a TV and DVD player hooked up and ready to go in the new house on moving day. Sure, we'd like to give each kid a job and teach responsibility, but often that can be too hard to do on one of life's most exhausting days. If possible, have the children stay with friends or relatives on the big day. (You might also consider having your pets stay at a boarding kennel or a friend's house for the day.)

Delegate. Give everyone in the family a list of tasks for which they will be responsible. This is particularly true if you have teenagers. Set it up several days before by calling a family meeting. Go down a list of what will need to be accomplished and then assign family members specific tasks.

Be considerate. On moving day, be considerate of both your old neighbors and the new ones. Don't let movers walk across neighbors' lawns or flower beds. Don't let the moving truck block anyone's driveway. Move after 9a.m. and before 8p.m. so you don't disturb anyone—new neighbors in particular.

Don't buy boxes and packing materials from the mover. They are overpriced. Storage companies have lower prices on their boxes and packing materials.

Stay in close communication with the moving company. If you've made a long distance move and are waiting on your truck with all your belongings, get on the phone, even if the truck is only one day late. If your furniture is late for several days, your movers should put you up in a hotel.

Check for breakage. Don't sign a receipt from the movers until you have examined the most important of your furnishings. If the movers are in a big rush to leave, write on the receipt, "approved only upon unpacking boxes." Then insist that you get a copy of the receipt that they take.

SMART FINANCIAL STEPS TO TAKE AFTER THE MOVE

Once you get into your new home, friends, family and your creditors may not be caught up with your new address yet. No mail? Think again! Your mailbox will be stuffed with all kinds of offers and solicitations. Home purchases are a matter of public record. Companies buy new home buyer lists inexpensively, giving vendors easy access to your address. Often, local newspapers even print the new home purchases. Some of the solicitations may seem too good to be true.

Here are the flyers to throw away:

Protect Your Home! This refers to mortgage life insurance and mortgage disability insurance. Even your own lender will send you this kind of offer. If you need life or disability insurance because you have dependents, consider low-cost, high-quality term life insurance.

Faster Mortgage Payoff! Here is a firm that offers for a fee to do what you can do for free. You already have the option of paying biweekly, thereby making 26 payments each year rather than 24. This does take eight years off your mortgage term. If these letters cause you to call your lender and ask for the biweekly option, then they've done you a service. Don't pay solicitors for a two-minute phone call you can make for free.

Refinance at Lower Rates! You just financed! Don't consider refinancing unless the interest rate is a full point lower than what you're currently paying. Mortgage rates just do not drop that far in a matter of weeks or months. Calculate how many months it will take you to recoup the cost of refinancing.

We'll Protect Your Home for Life! This kind of solicitation offers to file your house as a "homestead" for you. A portion of your home's equity can be protected from lawsuits when this document is in place. This document can be attained for free from your county recorder's office. In most states, you can even download it and fill it out online. Once again, do it yourself for free!

Consider Electronic Mortgage Payments

Most mortgage lenders have programs where your payment can be taken automatically from your bank account. Take advantage of this convenience to keep your credit squeaky clean. Being late can affect your credit standing and even cost more money with late penalties. If your mortgage lender does not have their own electronic payment program, chances are you can set up automatic payments through your online banking system.

Rebuild Your Emergency Reserve

A new home purchase has a way of wiping your finances out. Instead of spending every last dime on stuff for the new house, build a three-month emergency cash fund. Build that account to the equivalent of six months expenses. Staying out of malls and away from catalogs will help keep your spending in check. Besides, you most likely have many years to fix up and decorate your home. Spread the remodeling joy over time. You don't have to fill every nook and cranny of the home this year.

Keep Receipts for All Home Improvements

Make a special file now for all home improvement expenses and try to get all relevant receipts in there.

Most Importantly ...

Moving can be stressful, but if you use our worksheets, all of the tasks will fall into place for you. Organize early by making a list of all that needs to be done and get help from friends and family. Remember, it takes more than one person to move a whole family of belongings. Choose moving companies affiliated with the Better Business Bureau. Most of all, try to look at the moving process as an adventure rather than a horror. This will be one of the most memorable days of your life.

MOVING COMPANY CONTACT INFORMATION WORKSHEET

Use this worksheet to compare moving companies in your area and to make note of what their references have said about them.

	Company #1	Company #2	Company #3	Company #4
Name of Company				
Contact's Name				
Company Address				
Phone Number				
Email Address				
Web Address				
How much do you charge?				
What is your cancellation policy?				
Do you carry insurance?				
What happens if something breaks?				
When are you available?				
Reference #1 Name Phone number				
Reference #2 Name Phone number				
Reference #3 Name Phone number				

Use the following three worksheets to keep track of the people/companies that you must notify of your new address.

Organization/Individual	Name	Notified
Accountant		
Attorney		
Bank		
Catalogs		
Credit Card Company #1		
Credit Card Company #2		
Department Store		

Government Agencies	Name	Notified
DMV		
Post Office		
Social Security		
Voter Registration		

Insurance	Name	Notified
Auto		
Home		
Health		
Other:		

Lenders	Name	Notified
Mortgage		
Personal Loan		
Trust Deeds		

Investments	Name	Notified
Investment Manager		
Broker		
Online Investment Service		
Savings/CDs		
Partnerships		

Magazines/Newspapers	Name	Notified
Magazine #1		
Magazine #2		
Magazine #3		
Newspaper #1		
Newspaper #2		

Medical	Name	Notified
Chiropractor		
Dentist		
Ophthalmologist		
Family Doctor		
Specialist		
Pharmacy		
Therapist		
Veterinarian		

Religious Organization	Name	Notified
Church		
Charity		

Schools	Name	Notified
School #1		
School #2		

Miscellaneous	Name	Notified
Tenants		
Other:		
Other::		
Other:		
Other:		
Other:		
Other:		
Other:		
Other:		
Other:		
Other:		
Other:		
Other:		
Other:		
Other:		
Other:		
Other:		
Other:		
Other:		
Other:		
Other:		

SERVICE CANCELLATION WORKSHEET

Use this worksheet to keep track of the services that you must cancel before or after your move.

Service	Name	Notified
Cable		
Carpet Cleaner		
Drinking Water		
Phone		
Fuel Oil		
Garbage		
Gas & Electric		
House Cleaning		
Internet Provider		
Lawn Service		
Newspaper		
Pest Control		
Pool/Spa		
Sewer		
Telephone, Local		
Telephone, Long distance		
Telephone, Cell		
Water		
Water Softener		
Other:		

Here is a list of all the things you have to do to officially establish yourself at your new address. Check each box when completed, beginning two to four weeks before your move.

☐ Start saving boxes and other packing materials.

☐ Put in a "Change of Address" notification at the post office.

☐ As you receive bills in the mail, fill out the change of address area.

☐ Call the gas and electric company.

☐ Call the water company.

☐ Call your cable or satellite company.

☐ Call your Internet service provider.

☐ Call around to movers and find the right one for you.

☐ Make a list of friends and family who will need your new address, phone number and email address. This is most easily and inexpensively done via email.

☐ Find a place in the garage for the things you do not plan on taking with you when you move. Start separating those items now.

☐ Plan a date for a garage sale.

☐ Check school schedule and enrollment dates.

☐ Have school records transferred from old to new school.

☐ Sort belongings into those you want to transport yourself and those you want the mover to take.

☐ Notify magazines and other subscriptions of your change of address.

☐ Notify all your credit card companies of your change of address.

☐ Gather any personal records you want from doctors, dentists, lawyers and accountants.

☐ Find a new bank and transfer accounts.

☐ Pay all outstanding bills.

☐ Cancel newspaper or water deliveries.

☐ Arrange for someone to help watch your children on moving day.

☐ Order newspaper subscription for your new address.

THE FIRST WEEK IN YOUR NEW HOME CHECKLIST

Once you are in your new home, consider the following:

- ☐ Childproof your home, if necessary.
- ☐ Make a fire evacuation plan.
- ☐ Test security and smoke alarms.
- ☐ Get local emergency numbers and post them.
- ☐ Recycle or store moving boxes.
- ☐ Change door locks.
- ☐ Establish a file for all of your home and appliance warranties.
- ☐ Start or join a neighborhood program.
- ☐ File all of your real estate transaction documents.

PART 8:

NEW TRENDS IN REAL ESTATE

NOTES

IS A NONTRADITIONAL HOME RIGHT FOR YOU?

Knowing some current trends will help you make the wisest, most appropriate—and most exciting—purchase on what is likely the largest financial transaction you'll make in your life. The housing industry is showing some great ingenuity and cosmic consciousness.

THE DIGITAL HOME

A prototype of a leading software company's futuristic digitized home has the usual B-grade science fiction movie amenities: a pleasant voice to welcome you home as your key card trips the front door locks, a front door camera that beams an image of any visitors stopping by to your cell phone as you drive on the highway 20 miles away; phone-activated security, heating and cooling systems. Of course, this digital home's televisions are networked with the computers, stereo system and even the phones. The whole goal is to make everything automatic, easy and accessible from remote locations.

Central in this new digitalized future home is what is known as "radio frequency identification" (RFID) tags. These aren't just headline-grabbing gimmicks. Many futurists believe these "smart tags" will come equipped with most consumer products within the next ten years. Complete with their own antennas and miniscule batteries, RFID tags are the elaborate bar codes of the future. Once stored in your digital refrigerator, grocery items will keep track of themselves and notify you when you need to purchase more. You will be able to call or email your refrigerator from work to see if you have three eggs for that brownie mix or not. This digital kitchen will have a counter panel with the ability to read food packages. If you plunk down a package of chicken parts on it, the computer reads the tag and then displays a nice chicken fricassee recipe on a nearby screen.

These tags are also slated to be included in clothing, thereby increasing the IQs of the closest as well. Future digital closets will help consumers keep on top of what clothes are in the laundry, the dry cleaners and what's actually clean. They even go so far as to suggest which top matches a pair of slacks. Radio frequency identification tags will play a part in all of our lives in the coming years.

For now, the digital options available for builders (both commercial and residential) allow you to:

- Network your personal computers, stereos, televisions and other audio/video equipment so they can send videos, music, messages and documents throughout the house with just the touch of a button.

- Manage lighting, heating and cooling systems from anywhere in the home, perhaps from a graphic, flat-panel screen.

- Store electric, water and gas utility data and use the information to help you make decisions about the usage of each utility.

- Run multiple systems: lighting, electrical and heating or cooling from one or several remote controls.

- Use wireless sensors to create an integrated security system.

- Raise and lower window shades throughout the house by remote control.

These options are increasingly being offered in brand-new homes. If you're building your own home, there are businesses that are happy to come out and install as much wireless or broadband technology as you can dream up.

Before discussing your tech needs with your builder, stop by the Digital Living Network Alliance website at www.dlna.org. This is an organization made up of hundreds of electronics manufacturers working hard toward "interoperability" of their products. Their goal is to create a seamless environment for sharing music, movies, email, documents and anything else that can be converted into a computer file.

If you are interested in products like these, look for the words "interoperability" in their description or the Digital Living Network Alliance seal when shopping.

WARNING! With all of these devices connected, it's easy to see how homes will need what may seem like a ridiculous amount of bandwidth. Video and audio will be flowing over cable lines at the same time and from several different sources as members of the household compete for bandwidth. Without decent bandwidth, music can falter and videos will break up and/or freeze. Some industry experts are encouraging builders to install cables that can accommodate one gigabyte of bandwidth. If you want a high tech home, ask the builder about the bandwidth of the cable they're planning to install. Ask their rationale behind their choice and make sure you agree with it, particularly if you are a digital lover. For a while, cable will deliver the best connectivity, but wireless (where devices will be linked without cable) is not too many years away.

GOING GREEN – ENERGY-EFFICIENT AND HEALTH-CONSCIOUS HOMES

While the digital home makes living easier and more entertaining, the "green home" makes it more meaningful. Environmentalism is no longer a fringe phenomenon. In fact, there will soon be more builders creating green homes than those who aren't. These kinds of homes use energy-efficient and health-protecting materials. The building industry has found that consumers are enthusiastic about homes that increase indoor air quality and use water and energy more efficiently.

The biggest reason to go green, builders claim, is that it is the right thing to do. Considering the savings on energy bills that last over the lifetime of the house, builders' requests for a premium for green housing is not that outrageous. Your costs will be up-front, but you will save over your lifetime.

California Goes Green

In 2004, California Governor Arnold Schwarzenegger signed a "Green Building Action Plan" that committed the government to building structures that are highly energy efficient. Part of the plan stipulates that all new and renovated state-owned and state-funded facilities strive to earn the Silver LEED (Leadership in Energy and Environmental Design) certification from the U.S. Green Building Council (USGBC). As California goes, so goes the country. California is the first state to write energy conservation into legislation, but it is not long before others will begin doing the same.

In 2004, the National Association of Home Builders developed the Model Green Home Building Guidelines in order to provide practical standards and minimums for resource-efficient, cost-effective home building. Builders that comply with these standards earn the designation "green." These guidelines focus on the following areas:

Energy Efficiency: Today's average home uses almost 23 percent less energy each day than a home built before 1960. New homeowners want that number to get even lower. By incorporating the right windows, doors and insulation, energy efficiency can be greatly enhanced. With homeowners using less energy, power plant emissions are decreasing, improving air quality in the environment.

Indoor Air Quality: This aspect always turns up next on the list of environmental concerns when someone purchases a new home. In areas where there are high pollen and pollutant densities, it's particularly important. Special filtration systems reduce the amount of both pollens and pollutants in the inside air.

Global Impact: Some green builders keep the whole planet in mind when they choose paints that won't affect the ozone layer and plants that grow naturally in the area and conserve water. There are many ways green builders are trying to protect the air quality, the ozone and the natural habitat.

Lot Development and Building: Builders strive to reduce erosion, preserve trees and local ecosystems and reduce waste during the building process.

Homeowner Education: A builder can set up a green home for a client, but if that client doesn't know how to operate the heating and cooling system or regulate indoor versus outdoor air, the builders' efforts are wasted. Improper and inadequate maintenance can ruin everyone's best intentions in a green home. Not changing air filters and using cleaning products high in dangerous chemicals can reduce the indoor air quality. For a home to qualify as green, the builder takes on the responsibility of making sure the homeowner knows how to operate and maintain the equipment and reduce the level of toxins they introduce into the environment.

Water Efficiency: Homeowners normally use 64 gallons of water each day to run the average home. The Model Green Home Building Guidelines demonstrate how builders can install water-efficient products and choose native landscaping options to reduce that amount to 20 gallons.

Conserving Building Materials: The Green Home Building Guidelines include reducing job site waste and using building materials like engineered wood products that put leftover materials to work. Natural resources are depleted at a slower rate.

For more information, you can find the Green Building Initiative at www.thegbi.org on the Internet. The Green Building Initiative is an alliance of builders, researchers and consumers that focus on energy-efficient, healthier and environmentally conscious construction. Another similar organization is the United States Green Building Council, also made up of building industry and environmental issues leaders. Their website is www.usgbc.org.

Green homes are becoming more prevalent because the number of green products (appliances and energy systems, mostly) to fill them with is increasing exponentially as well. Energy Star is a government-backed program helping businesses and individuals create and use products that conserve energy, protect the environment and improve both indoor and outdoor air quality. Their site (www.energystar.gov) not only lists these products, but also offers ideas on how to make your home more energy efficient.

If you are building a home, you can get an Energy Star designation for your home if it meets certain guidelines. It could qualify for lower electric rates and gas bills. If your builder claims that their homes are Energy Star homes, they too have met some requirements set up by this organization. These homes must meet minimum standards for effective insulation, high performance windows, tight ducts and construction, efficient heating and cooling equipment and lighting fixtures (like fluorescent bulbs) that reduce energy use. Once building is complete, the organization sends out a "Home Energy Rater" to make sure the home qualifies for the Energy Star designation.

The Energy Star website also provides lists of builders in your area familiar with the Energy Star program. You can perform a quick home energy analysis of your home on their website. You'll need pertinent information like the home's square footage and your utility bills. Most of all, you can find Energy Star approved appliances, lighting fixtures and bulbs, heating and cooling apparatus and more listed there, along with the local stores that carry them. If you're concerned about the environment around you and the well-being of the ecosphere itself, a green home may be for you.

TRENDS IN ROOM AND HOME DESIGN

Digital and green homes aren't the only newcomers shaking up the housing industry. Home sizes and designs are changing as well. Homes are growing larger and larger. In 1975 the size of the average home was 1,645 square feet. In 2005 it was 2,434 and the ever-increasing square footage trend does not seem to be stopping any time soon. Between 1975 and 2005, the number of newly built homes with four or more bedrooms rose from 21 percent to almost 40 percent. And big houses tend to attract big cars. Since 1991, the number of three-car garages doubled from 10 percent to 20 percent in 2005. The new homes get larger and larger, even as actual lot size decreases.

Bigger homes mean bigger individual rooms. Architects and builders report that consumers are continuing in the nesting phase with kitchens and bathrooms getting larger and going more upscale. Consumers are demanding larger pantry space, high-end appliances and granite countertops in more spacious kitchens. Also in response to demand, builders are putting heated floors and fireplaces in large master bathrooms. Some homeowners are even requesting two separate showers in master bathrooms.

The upscale trend pervades many aspects of the home. Central air conditioning seems to be a must-have in homes in all four regions of the United States. Ceilings are stretching higher too. Standard ceiling height has traditionally been around eight feet. More than half of all new homes built in 2005 had ceilings that were nine feet or higher on the first floor.

IS A NONTRADITIONAL HOME RIGHT FOR YOU?

Trends in home exteriors are turning out to be just as fickle as interior trends. The first casualty: decks, which are starting to go the way of the dinosaur. Instead, front patios and front porches where people can gather and interact with neighbors are rising in popularity. While the number of two-story homes has nearly doubled in the last 30 years, split-level homes are out, way out. The number of one-story homes has declined from 65 percent in 1975 to 44 percent in 2005. Vinyl siding has now actually replaced brick and wood as the most popular exterior.

The above information shows you what home amenities are striking buyers' fancies these days. In ten years, there could be a whole other slew of features each homeowner has to have. You may not have thought of some of them. You may not like any of them. Whichever way you believe, it's good to know what's out there. Please remember trends have nothing to do with your preferences.

DEMOGRAPHICS: CHANGING STYLES TO MATCH THE NEW BUYERS

In the last two decades, builders designed homes for families happy with kitchens appended to family rooms and a bedroom for each child. They now have to revisit their ideal of the typical buyer. America's population of those over 50 will reach 100 million by the year 2010, and builders are trying to carve their own shares of that large population.

The buzzword for this aging population is now "active." Post middle-agers are working longer, exercising at greater rates and interacting more socially and culturally than their parents did. Many of these 50-plus consumers no longer have children living at home

Home buyers in this demographic are asking more of builders and the existing homes they're considering for purchase. For instance, small bathrooms cause big problems with accessibility. The good news is that most small bathrooms can be modified without spending a fortune to accommodate wheelchairs. Some master bathrooms may even have enough space with a modest redesign. It may be surprising to realize that the typical master bath in the United States constructed from the late 1940s until the last decade has been about 5'x7' or 8'x7'. Specialists in accessible design say a 5'x8' space is generally considered the minimum space a homeowner needs to fit an accessible toilet, sink and roll-in shower. A 5'x5' space is the absolute minimum for a sink and toilet.

When you evaluate your home to see if it makes sense to remodel, consider this checklist recommended by the Certified Aging-in-Place Specialists (CAPS):

☐ A master bedroom and bath on the first floor
☐ A low or no-threshold entrance to the home with an overhang
☐ Lever door handles
☐ No change in levels on the main floor
☐ Bright lighting in all areas
☐ A low maintenance exterior
☐ Nonslip flooring at the main entryway
☐ An open floor plan, especially in the kitchen and dining areas
☐ Handrails at all steps

Moving to More Urban Areas

With children out of the house, many older couples can scale down to the smaller units more prevalent in the urban areas. Because condominium maintenance is so much lower, the 50-plus Baby Boomers find a pleasing, less stressed life in homes without yards and the continual repair demands. Traveling becomes easier when all you have to do is ask the doorman to gather your mail for you. Well-known as individualistic, these Baby Boomers find the option of public transportation in urban areas appealing. Companies are building to meet the demands of empty nesters with active, engaged lifestyles.

Despite rumors that older consumers gravitate toward warmer places as they retire, research shows that people tend to retire in the communities where they've lived and worked for decades. This is especially true if their children remain in the area, and they are connected to a community of friends. While retirees may scale down, they don't necessarily move to an entirely new community, sunny days or not. Moving to the urban section of the city they grew up in could count as all the change Boomers need.

It's not just the 50-plus Boomers that builders are catering to these days. Other populations can enjoy the attention they'll start getting from builders now as their ranks swell. The nuclear family is on the wane. From 1994 until 2002, the number of unmarried women buying homes for the first time increased by 30 percent. The two other groups that account for the fastest growing home buying populations are minorities and immigrants. In 1980, only 17 percent of minorities owned homes. That share is expected to increase to 30 percent by 2010 and 34 percent by 2020. This means that minorities will fuel 66 percent of all new home sales over the next two decades. With the potential profits locked in this group, builders, real estate agents and mortgage lenders will certainly begin marketing to them, making homes more appealing and easier to acquire.

SOLUTIONS TO THE AFFORDABILITY CRISIS

The run-up in housing prices that occurred over the last decade has prompted local and national government bodies, businesses and even building associations to find ways to make housing more affordable. There is pressure on government bodies and businesses to make housing less expensive. Some legislation is in the works to do just that. Businesses have been responding as well. It's only in their best interests as their workforce will need to have housing if they are to have stable, productive and content employees.

Aside from governments longing to get their citizens and businesses wanting to get workers into homes, builders are exploring their own ways to create less expensive housing. They, too, have to make these changes in order to find new markets full of first-time buyers, to get this class into the housing market. The low wage employment sector is growing at a faster rate than the middle- and high-wage sectors. There will be more low-wage families looking for homes. Builders can make profits from this group, and hopefully they will find creative ways to do so.

NEW TRENDS IN MORTGAGE LENDING

The increase in the numbers of minorities, immigrants and single women as first-time home buyers, coupled with the inflation in house prices has finally prompted lenders to come up with mortgage products targeting these groups. Demographics have shifted greatly, and lenders have to find ways to get more buyers into homes to make more sales. This means making mortgages easier and less expensive to acquire. Look for the following trends in mortgage lending:

- Borrowers can present funds and assets from family members and others as part of their down payments or income. In other words, lenders are facilitating familial contributions to first-time home buyers.

- Cosigners now do not have to live in the house being purchased. Parents and other family members can more easily help children buy their first home.

- Mortgage lenders are looking upon money kept in a community savings fund or cash or other nontraditional ways of pooling money as legitimate sources of funds.

- Lenders are loosening their credit score policies. In fact, some will now look at rental histories and proof of consistent utility, telephone and cable payments along with credit history to determine creditworthiness.

• Potential income from renting one of the rooms in the home can count toward income qualifying the buyer to purchase the home. This hasn't been the case until now.

• Lenders will consider hard-to-document, cash income from jobs such as home maintenance, cleaning services, child care and other employment as legitimate, given other documentation or backup from employers.

• Down payments may possibly go as low as 1 percent of the home's purchase price.

While these trends are not in place at all lending organizations, many lending organizations are looking at them. Lenders have to make changes like this or they will have no new markets to sell money to.

Changes in the mortgage industry now favor those buyers who typically have a tougher time qualifying for a loan. Money is becoming easier to acquire, as evidenced by the prevalence of adjustable rate mortgages, two-step loans and balloon loans.

Another indicator of lenders' willingness to deal is the increase in the number of loans to "sub-prime" borrowers, those with blemished credit histories. If you have spotty credit, you no longer need to feel you'll get a hard time when applying for loans. Mortgage lenders are trying to find ways to guarantee they'll get their money while making these transactions.

Families who put 20 percent down on a home with a fixed rate mortgage—once the norm—will become increasingly rare. Now, mortgage lenders and builders are scrambling to meet the needs of many niches, most of whom are not the typical nuclear family with two children and a white collar income stream. If you fit in one of these other niches, it is your time to go to your mortgage lender and ask for as much as you can get. You are now the most sought-after borrower.

Most Importantly ...
Knowing what housing trends are occurring can benefit you. There are exciting options available today and in the future. At the same time, a trend does not mean a must-have! Remember your own priorities when shopping for homes.

NOTES

PART 9:

GRAPH PAPER AND FURNITURE TEMPLATES

NOTES

USING THE GRAPH PAPER AND FURNITURE TEMPLATES

Take the measurements of each room in your home and draw the walls of each room on the graph paper provided, noting the locations of doors (and the direction of the swing), windows, plumbing and electrical outlets. The scale is designed so that one grid square equals one square foot (1:1) or each line is equal to one linear foot.

Please note: for the furniture templates to reflect how your furniture will appear in the actual space, be sure to follow the 1:1 scale provided. Measurements will be incorrect if you change the scale when using the furniture templates.

From this point, you can measure all of your furnishings and items you want in the space. Pop out the furniture template corresponding to the approximate size of your furniture. Place the templates in the space you created on the grid paper. Move them around and experiment with how they fill the space. Do you have too much furniture, too little, or just the right amount? Check to make sure each item fits where you thought it would. Ensure lamps are placed close enough to electrical outlets, and that nothing blocks the doors. It can be fun to see your rooms from a bird's eye view, and very helpful as well. Allow three feet between furniture for walking.

WHY THIS IS IMPORTANT

There are five good reasons to take the time to perform this essential exercise:

1. The excitement of a room makeover sometimes skips over the practical aspect of how it will affect the functionality of a room. If the room has two or three entrances, will there be freedom of movement as people pass through, or is the configuration looking more like an obstacle course? If you want to remake the sitting area into a media room, is there enough space to install that 52-inch plasma television and still have sufficient room to sit at a comfortable distance from the screen? Graphically laying out the elements can avert disappointment when the job is done.

2. A rough layout can tell you if your furniture is proportionate to the scale of the room. For example, if you have chosen delicate or minimalist furnishings, but the room includes high ceilings and an expansive square footage addition, your furniture will be lost in the large room. Conversely, maybe you picked large overstuffed chairs and a large sofa or sectional. Cramming these large pieces of furniture into a new smaller area will crowd the room. Sometimes covering an entire wall with a custom cabinet solves storage and electronic equipment problem, but overpowers the rest of the room.

3. This exercise can tell you if you have too many or too few furnishings in the room. Let's say you wanted that minimalist look in the new room. Placing the furniture templates of all the items you want in the room in a scaled representation of how the room will look when done helps you to immediately see if it will appear too cluttered to convey a minimalist impression. Or, if you wanted the country or cottage look, you may discover you need a few additional pieces to comfortably fill the space.

4. This exercise can eliminate the "Oops!" factor. By noting on your drawing the precise location of all windows, doors (as well as which way the doors swing), vents in the floor, available power, and existing plumbing, you can situate furnishings the way you want without interfering with fixed elements. It may also indicate where additional power or plumbing will be required to suit your needs.

5. Graphically laying out what you want to see can focus your thoughts. This is where the subtle "tweaking" of your ideas can save you a lot of frustration, time and certainly money in purchasing the wrong size of furniture. It is not uncommon for the plan you ultimately adopt to differ from the first ideas that sparked your desire to improve your home. The more you refine your idea before you go on a shopping spree, the more money you will save.

SAMPLE MASTER BEDROOM

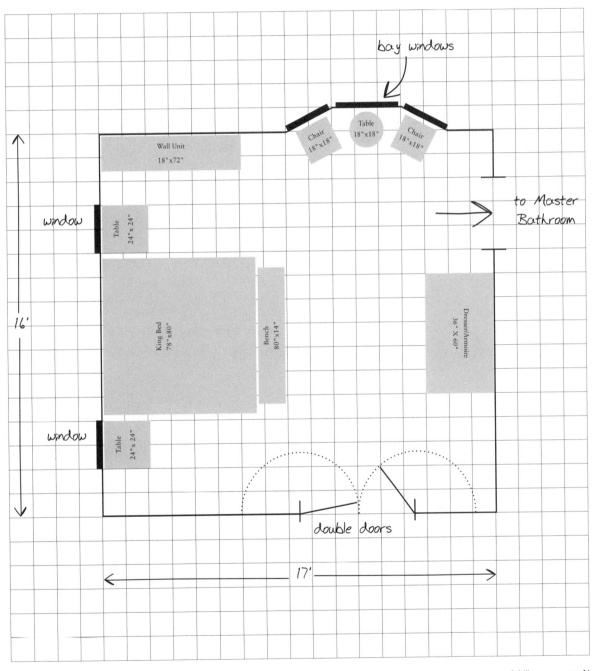

1/4" measures 1'

NOTES

Make copies of this sheet as needed for each room of your home.　　　1/4" measures 1'

GRAPH PAPER

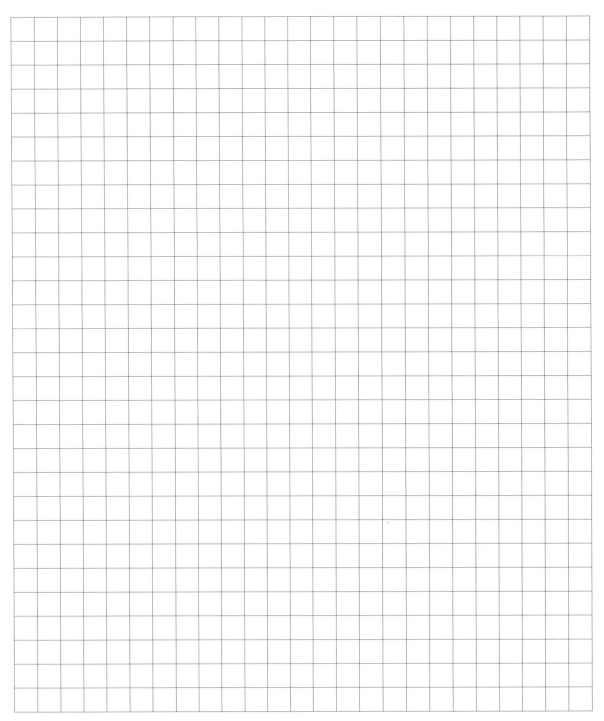

Make copies of this sheet as needed for each room of your home.   1/4" measures 1'

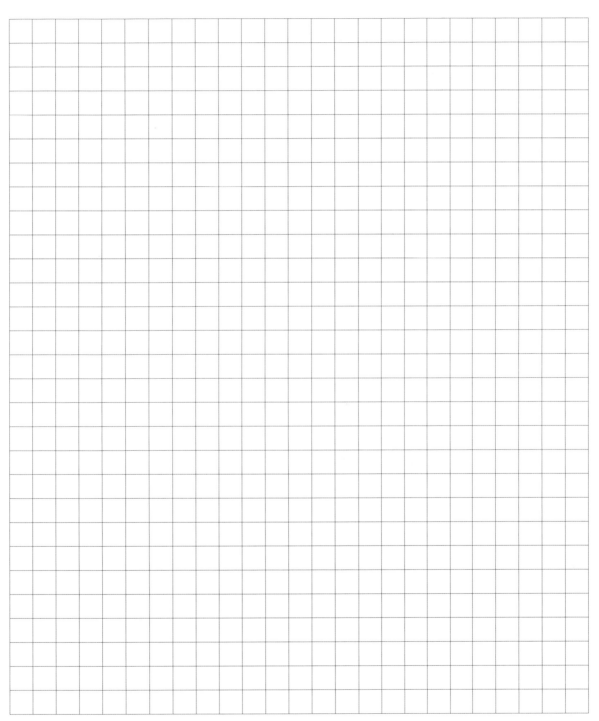

Make copies of this sheet as needed for each room of your home. 1/4" measures 1'

GRAPH PAPER

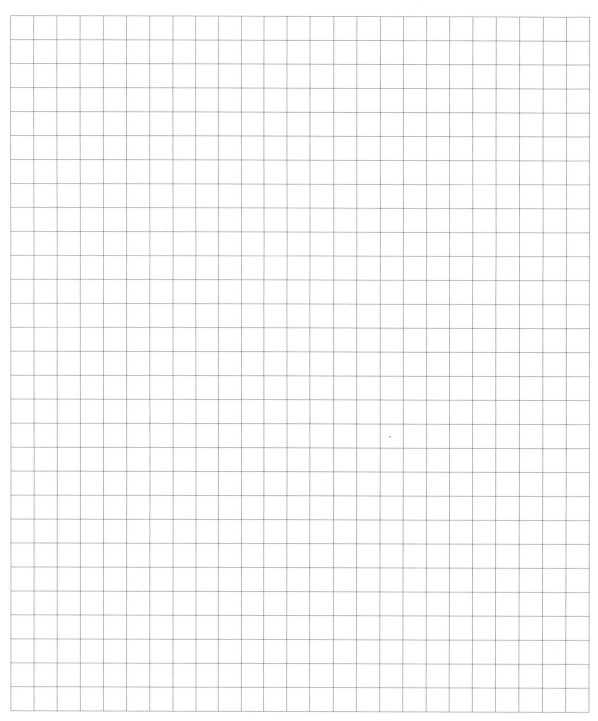

Make copies of this sheet as needed for each room of your home.   1/4" measures 1'

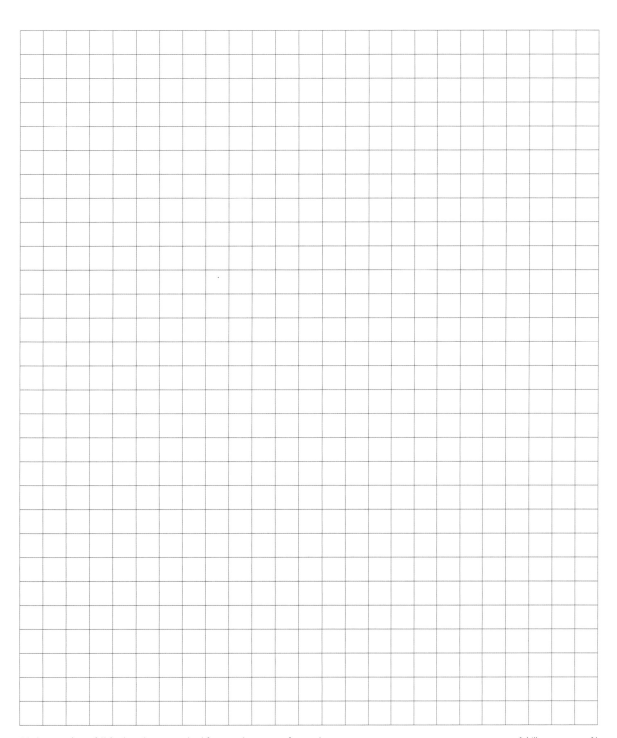

Make copies of this sheet as needed for each room of your home.   1/4" measures 1'

GRAPH PAPER

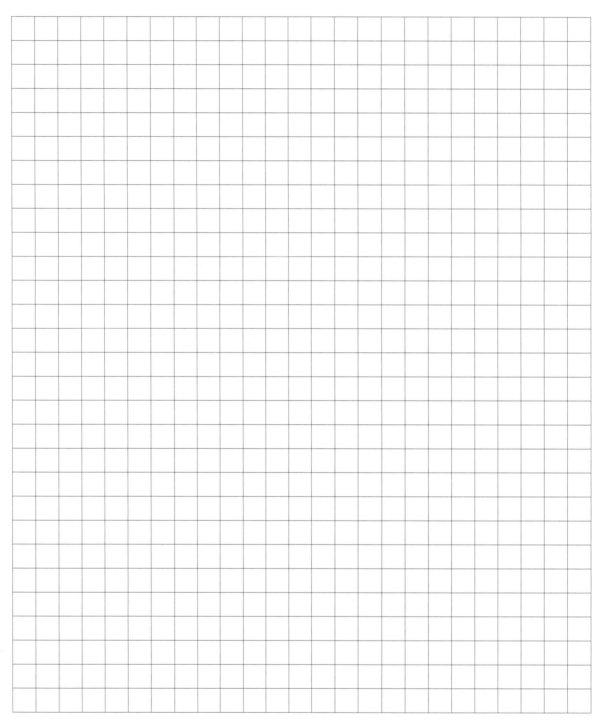

Make copies of this sheet as needed for each room of your home.   1/4" measures 1'

Make copies of this sheet as needed for each room of your home.   1/4" measures 1'

GRAPH PAPER

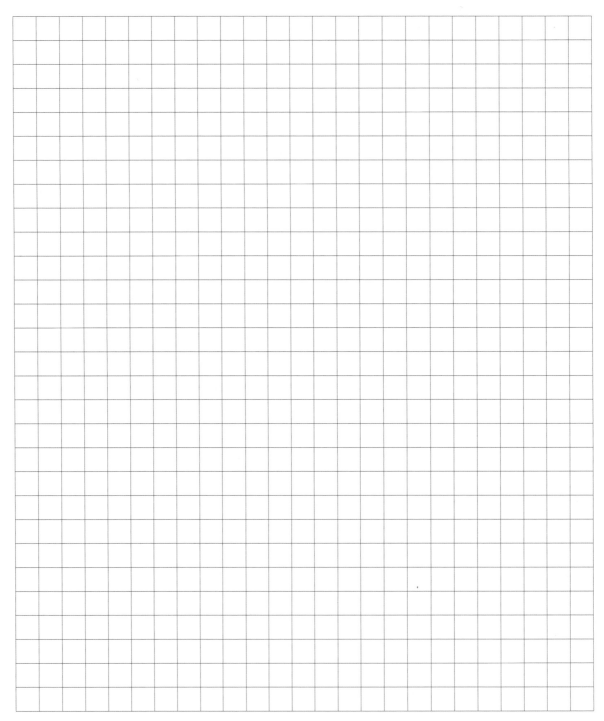

Make copies of this sheet as needed for each room of your home.   1/4" measures 1'

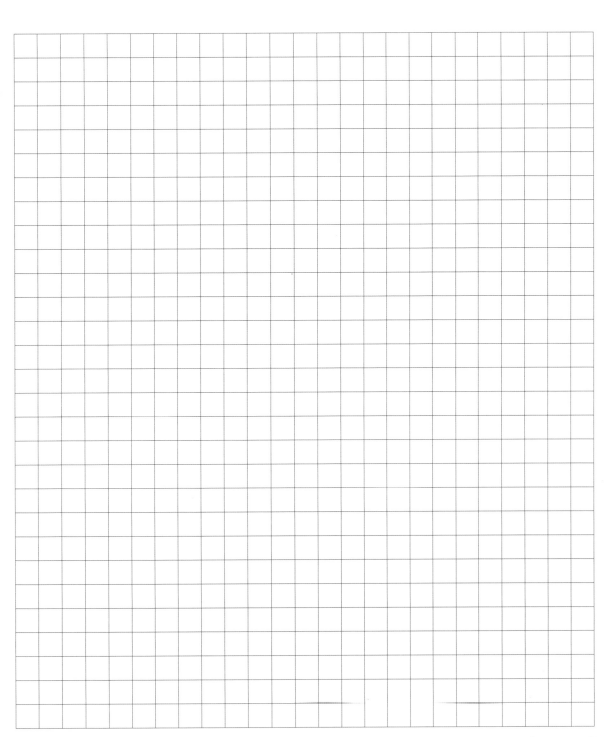

Make copies of this sheet as needed for each room of your home.   1/4" measures 1'

GRAPH PAPER

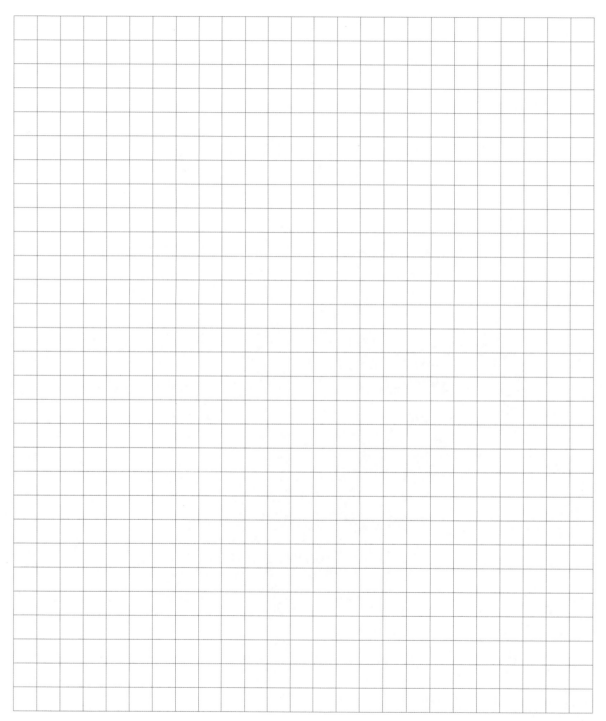

1/4" measures 1'

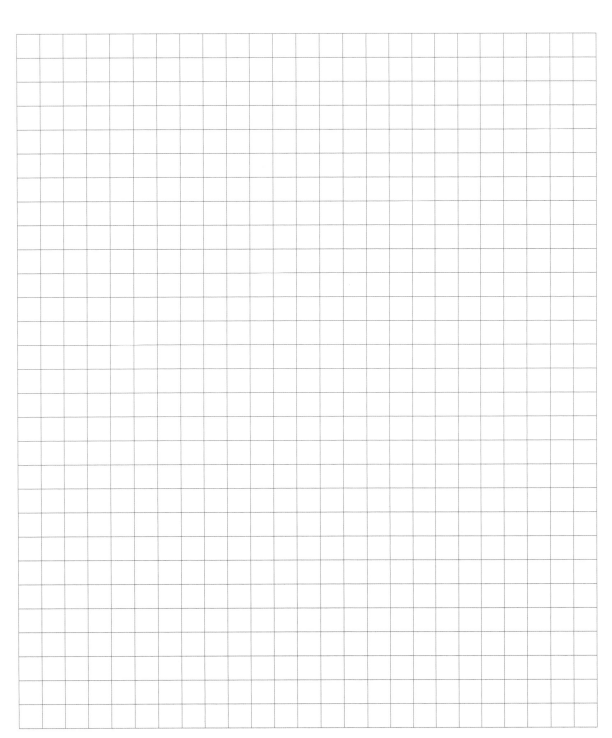

Make copies of this sheet as needed for each room of your home. 1/4" measures 1'

GRAPH PAPER

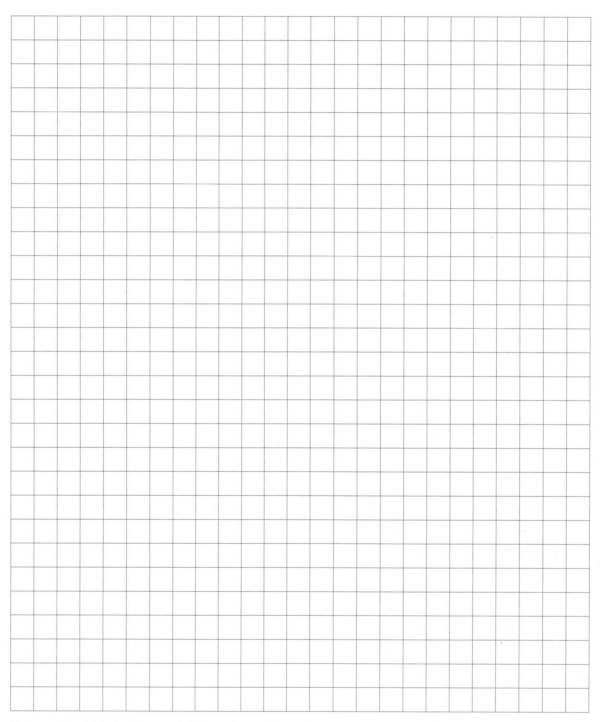

Make copies of this sheet as needed for each room of your home.   1/4" measures 1'